Overheard at the Day Care

by

Charles M. Conver

DORRANCE PUBLISHING CO., INC.
PITTSBURGH, PENNSYLVANIA 15222

ISBN # 0-8059-3821-4
Printed in the United States of America

First Printing

For information or to order additional books, please write:
Dorrance Publishing Co., Inc.
643 Smithfield Street
Pittsburgh, Pennsylvania 15222
U.S.A.

Dedication

*My wife Marion tells me this book could be
read aloud...with appropriate expressions on
the face and changing voices as the "script"
may indicate! Upon reflection, she has a
point. This book is dedicated to children
everywhere, including the child in you, which
happily emerges every now and then.*
C.M.C.

Contents

Foreword

Those of you who now have or have had little children, or have been fortunate enough to be around them from time to time perhaps will enjoy and appreciate this book. I hope I have captured in the following anecdotes the often candid remarks of youngsters—reflecting their sweet innocence and love, their frankness and honesty, their natural self-centeredness at times, and their delightful reactions to people, places, and things.

I was employed as a teacher at the Viers Mill Child Care Center, Viers Mill Baptist Church in Silver Spring, Maryland, for fourteen plus years. The children in the Center are ages two through five, and they come from all walks of life. Also, because we are located in suburban Washington D.C., we have a cosmopolitan representation of different cultures. At one time our Director, Maxine Holden, did a quick survey of the countries represented and discovered that, of an enrollment of sixty children, there were twenty-seven countries represented including the United States. Let me say, however, my experience with children convinces me that children are pretty much the same regardless of their origins.

Shortly after I began my work at Viers Mill, I realized that these dear children gave me so much and made my life richer and more meaningful. I came to feel very strongly that their remarks were too precious to be heard only by me and perhaps a few other lucky people, so I decided to put them into a book, *Overheard at the Day Care*. While I was at work I began to write down the gist of remarks I heard...frequently, but not always, addressed to me, and then I stuffed them into my pocket. Later at home and while the details were fresh in my memory, I completed the vignettes on 3–by–5 cards and filed them in my brand new, green file box for the time I would write my book!

I have identified the children by first names only even though there might have been two children with the same name at the same time. I've tried to clarify which child is which by telling the age of the child or the group he/she belonged in as well as the time of year the incidents occurred.

I trust this won't pose any problems to the readers. Hopefully, some parents will recognize their children, and that is my main purpose for them...to remember their children at a given time and place and rejoice in the moments of reflection as I do over and over again.

The stories are loosely arranged by subject matter, and no concerted effort has been made to be chronological. As I shared my plans for this book with the staff at the Center, every now and then Maxine, an earlier director, and other co-workers reported gems of conversations they had "overheard."

It wasn't long before other sources became available to me—from parents of the children, Sunday School teachers, my family members, friends—all sharing comments about their children in bath tubs, cars, at restaurants, parties, family reunions, at nap time, on the telephone, or before TV screens, or as my grandson Isaac might say, "wherever." I've decided to reserve those delightful gems for another book.

I hope you will derive as much enjoyment from reading these tidbits as I have had in writing them. Surely the world needs laughter and is a happier place because of the remarks of our dear children.

1   Picturesque Speech - To Be Sure

I guess basically the most delightful thing about little children is their vocabularies, which reflect not only their reactions to remarks of others but to situations they witness as well. So often they pick up words and casually add them to their repertoire. Then, in the most interesting ways, they come out in conversations. The result is picturesque to say the least.

The following are some beguiling moments overheard at the day care which I hope reflect the above thoughts.

On the playground one sunny afternoon, at the top of the hill next to the sandbox, I sat on a chair watching the children having fun in the sand. Presently Amy bounded up the hill and joined me, standing behind my chair. "Let's play, Charles," she coaxed.

"I'm a bit tired, Amy," was my response, "but I'll tell you a story, okay?" Amy smiled her approval, and I began the story about "The Three Little Pigs." I suddenly got the urge to take some liberties with the story, and playing the part of the wolf, I knocked on the back of the metal chair—three good raps. Then I imitated the wolf, "Little Pig, Little Pig, let me come in." "Not by the hair of my chinny-chin-chin," I squealed in a high-pitched voice. Then I threw my curve ball as once again my voice changed to that of the wolf. "Okay, if that's the way you want it!" I said disgustedly.

Amy frowned, thought a brief moment, and finally spoke up. In a very annoyed voice she asked, "Say, what kind of a wolf are you, anyway?"

It was nap time, and Doris, the senior teacher in the room, and I were relaxing a bit, having finally gotten all the children settled down on their cots. The varied sounds of their breathing as they slept were a welcome contrast to the boisterousness of a short time before. Suddenly Amy began to cry out in her sleep. I hastened to her cot, knelt down, and tried to be of some help. Stroking her forehead and dabbing at her tears, which by now were really flowing, I said softly, "There, there, Amy, it's allright. Everything is going to be fine. You're just having a nightmare." This caused her to pause in the midst of her tears. Frowning now, she said disgustedly, "That wasn't a nightmare. That was a daymare!" Then she settled down and presently dozed off once again.

On a rainy day when we were confined to the gym for our overall group activity, I suggested we go for a walk in the park. Several children responded to the suggestion, and as we walked I pointed out imaginary flowers, trees, birds, the lake, etc. Suddenly Ashwini said, "Look—some more flowers. And there's a bee!"

As the children stopped short I said, "Yes, I see. We've got to watch out for bees and yellow jackets!"

Her response was, "Yes—they're stinkers."

I was walking across the field late one afternoon, and as I approached the combined two and three-year-olds, the group spied me and rushed to meet me. Zachary was trailing behind the first few but was obviously very excited. "Charles, Charles, look what I found," he exclaimed. "A bony ball." He then plopped a nice, round pine cone in my hand.

It was pouring rain with much thunder and lightning, and little Johnny was very impressed. Suddenly, after a brilliant flash of lightning followed by rolls of thunder, he rushed excitedly to his father, who just happened to walk in the door on the way home from work. "Daddy, Daddy," he exclaimed, "God just took my picture!"

Allie's mother told me that her three-year-old daughter loved her bath time. In fact, it was often difficult to persuade her to get out of the tub. After one long soaking and much soaping on her part, Allie succumbed to her mother's urging to emerge from her bath. As her mother looked at the soap bar on the tub, Allie said, "I really feel very ZESTY today!"

Scott and Rory, oblivious to the other children, were running around the playground on the warm June afternoon when suddenly they spotted two crickets hopping along in the grass. Naturally that was the end of their romp as their eyes riveted on these strange but interesting creatures. As the crickets jumped—first one then the other—the boys moved along with them, very, very impressed. Maxine, the day care director, was nearby watching the boys. She had her ear cocked so as not to miss a word of their conversation. Out of the blue Scott said, "Let's stomp on them, Rory!"

In loud protest Rory responded, "No-o-o! You don't stomp on nature Mothers —never!"

One of the mothers whose child is in the day care told this story to the director at Easter time. It seems his class had a project of dyeing eggs by immersing them in little dishes of multi-colored dyes. At home that evening he said to his mother, "Mom, you know what?"

"What, dear?" was her reply.

"Today we killed eggs. We put them in dishes of color, and when they came out they died."

The teacher of the four-year-olds was giving out "smile" stickers to the children for good behavior. Suddenly one of them started to cry before the stickers were all passed out. "What is the matter with you?" asked the teacher.

Between sobs she replied, "Joe killed my smile!" There, lying on the floor, was the all-important but torn and wrinkled "smile" face.

Several of us were having an informal chit-chat under the huge oak tree on the playground that summer afternoon. In retrospect I can't remember who said what except for one comment which really made me smile. Pim was talking about her mother and dad. Suddenly she became really serious as she said, "Mother says Daddy and I eat too much junk food. But I like junk food. I'm a 'junkie'." (I couldn't tell from the tone of her voice whether she was bragging or complaining.)

I knew it was time to go in from the playground on one sweltering summer afternoon, when Meritese came up to me and exclaimed pitifully, "It's getting more and more thirsty, don't you think? I need a drink of water." Stifling a smile, I gave the order to line up, and we promptly marched inside to the water fountain. Of course Meritese got the first drink!

Jason was telling us about his recent day at the beach. We were all very interested because we had agreed a moment before that this hot day was a good day for the beach, and all of us wanted to be there so we could cool off in the water.

As Jason related one exciting experience after another, he finally came to the "big one." This was it. "I saw a horsey crab at the beach, but I didn't pick him up because he was still alive," he related to his spellbound audience. "And he had a sword he was waving around!"

There was an affirmative nodding of heads as several said, "I saw one at the beach, too, when I was there," or the usual, "Me, too!"

The new little boy from India was getting anxious as the day wore on. I kept reassuring him that his mother had not forgotten him and that she would be along pretty soon to pick him up just as the mothers or daddies of other boys and girls would be, too. I could see he was still anxious, but at the same time very brave. Finally he said, "Ven is the mothers of nobody coming?" His eyes were open wide.

"Soon, soon," I said softly, with a knowing smile as I knelt down and hugged him.

Our class was out walking around at nine o'clock, before the heat of the summer day made such a pleasure impossible. Nebelia, the other teacher with the rest of the class, was well behind us. After several hot, muggy days, yesterday had been a drizzly one. Now the sky was overcast, and we weren't sure when or if the sun would break through.

We were passing that wonderful hill in front of the church, and Ryan was holding my hand. "Charles," said Ryan, "can we run in the grass and roll down the hill?"

"Maybe later, Ryan," I said "Remember it was rainy yesterday, and the grass is still wet. We don't want to get our feet wet. Let's wait until the sun comes out and dries the grass. Okay?"

"The grass is still wet?" asked Ryan incredulously. As I looked up and pointed to the sky, Ryan's attention was riveted on the clouds which were moving swiftly, and every now and then the sun appeared briefly. There was a moment of silence and then Ryan, in a thoughtful mood, had this to say, "I guess the sun is taking a break."

Squeezing his hand I responded, "You're probably right."

After I had the fun and challenge of preparing the lunch for the day care on several occasions, the results appeared to be satisfactory—or more than that perhaps. Several of the children were moved to comment. Cynthia, a beautiful Latin American child, was especially complimentary. She came up to me in the gym and snuggled against me, murmuring softly and sweetly, "Charles, you're the best cooker we have."

At lunch time there is an adult at every table. She or he makes sure each child has a paper napkin and spoon by his/her paper plate. Then the adult pours milk into each of the paper cups and distributes them to the children. Ta was at my table for the first time, I believe. As usual he was attentive and not missing a thing. As I approached him with his cup of milk he said, "Charles, I can't drink milk. I'm illogic to milk." Needless to say, I was impressed by this revelation.

Another time I was chatting with a group of the kids on a Monday afternoon. The subject was week-end activities. Matin was on his favorite blue bike. He appeared to be even darker-skinned than he usually is. I said, "Matin, you look like you've been out in the sun. Did you go to a pool?"

"Yes," he said, "my daddy and I were at the pool, and he slapped my face."

"Oh," I replied, "were you naughty about something? You mean he slapped your beautiful suntan?"

His eyes sparkled as he concluded the conversation with the remark, "Yes, he slapped the sun right off my face."

There was a great day of hurly-burly, roughhouse playing under the tall, splendid oak tree behind the church. Suddenly Patti was going to each child and playfully punching each one. Zachary wasn't too happy about the prospect of being one of her victims, so he stood off on the periphery, obviously trying to avoid Patti but terribly curious about this new game. However, Patti was in a democratic mood, and Zachary's turn had come. Patti gently punched Zachary, who immediately came running up to me. In his peculiar, whining way he exclaimed, "Patti is giving me some punch, and I don't want it."

I suppose I shouldn't have been so surprised at Natasha's comments since the mole on my nose, along with the small silver filling on one of my front teeth, sooner or later is asked about by one or more of the children. Natasha was not an exception, so here it came again.

"Charles, what's that on your nose?"

I tried to be nonchalant. "Oh, that's just a mole."

"You're putting me on."

"No, I'm not. It's a mole."

"Well, how come it's on your nose?"

"I don't know. It just is, Natasha."

"Well, why isn't it on the ground?"

Now I was confused, so I asked, "Why should it be on the ground?"

After a brief pause and with a tone of meekness, the response came. "It should be on the ground in the woods, running with the rabbits."

I made light of this remark. "Oh, it should, should it?" (At the same time I was thinking, "At least that's a little different reaction than I'm used to getting.")

I was in the gym with the three-year-olds, and we were engaged in active play. I found myself the "chosen one" to receive all sizes of rubber balls being tossed to and fro. As I received them I bounced them around and then either tossed them or punched them at random. The children would respond by chasing after them, running back to me, and throwing them to me so that the whole procedure could begin again.

I couldn't help but notice that Kristen was on the sidelines, observing but obviously itching to get involved in the game herself. Kristen's mother had told me she had an infection that had caused her spleen to become enlarged, so she couldn't run around for awhile. With that information in mind, I went over to Kristen, intending to say something to encourage her. Before I could open my mouth she said. "I can't run because I've got a spleen in my tummy."

Erica was nearby and heard Kristen's comment. "Me, too," she said, "I've got a splinter in my toe." She sat down on the floor and proceeded to take her shoe off to show the evidence to her doubting teacher. I went along with the gesture, of course!

It was a Thursday morning and our turn to go to the nursing home to visit the patients and to sing for them. The children were walking in pairs along the street, happy as they could be and distracted constantly with everything they saw. Nelia and Turia, holding hands and moving along at a snail's pace in spite of the gentle but ever persistent prodding of one of the teachers, spied a jeep-like truck. "Ice cream truck, ice cream truck," they both exclaimed excitedly. Carlos, however, seemed a bit disgusted as he said, "That's not an ice cream truck! That's a gyp!"

Fortunately for the cook at the day care, by and large the children do not seem to be finicky eaters. However, one never knows when one of them will act up at the table.

One day recently, after a prayer of thanksgiving at the tables at lunch time, I passed out the different things on the menu for that day. The cook had toasted some brown bread with thick crusts, buttered it, and after cutting each piece in four, filled a plate for each table. The kids at my table seemed enthused to get some. They were all smiles and chattering among themselves. But as I approached Yefim he started to shake his head no. "Yefim," I exclaimed, "don't you want a piece?"

"Not me," said Yefim "I don't like all the skins on it!"

Again in the threes at group time we were sharing our weekend experiences. Apparently Michael had been away for several days at an amusement center. He was ecstatic over the rides he had gone on. His concluding remark was the highlight of our sharing that day. "I liked the holy coaster the best," he exclaimed, breaking out in a big grin. None of the kids batted an eye, but the teachers in the room were hard-pressed to stifle a laugh or a smile. But we did.

On a recent walk with the three-year-olds, the following conversation took place between Katie, Nicole, and myself:

Katie: "Charles, I had a lighting bug in my hand last night, and it glowed."

Charles: "That's nice. I bet it was fun."

Katie: "Yes...sometimes I like to put them in jars. (pause) They don't bite either."

Nicole: "Cause they don't have any teeth."

Katie: "Uh-huh. They don't have any teeth."

Nicole: "They can't talk either."

Katie: "No-o-o."

...and the conversation then changed to more mundane subjects.

Two-year-old Lee was talking to her teacher, Doris, about her weekend experience. One of the things she had done was to visit her doctor. "I got a stickler in my leg," she said, almost in a bragging tone.

Doris said, "You did, Lee, don't you mean the doctor gave you a needle—a shot in your leg?"

Lee said, "Oh, no. It was a stickler—a big, long one." Her tone of voice indicated it was what she said, and that was all there was to it. (And you better believe it!)

Chubby, adorable, two-year-old Sean was a part of a small group of very lively tots, beating the taller grass along the fence with sticks (a "no-no" activity, I might add!). I rushed over to reassert the rule with, I hope, restrained authority. "No, no," I called.

Suddenly Sean broke away from the dedicated group and hurried to my side in a frightened manner. As he drew closer I spied a gnat circling his head again and again. Close by me now, I became aware of Sean's plaintive cry, "There's a bug, bugging me!"

I was really surprised that afternoon in late October, when I arrived at the center and discovered that most of the children in the younger two-year-olds had runny noses. Doris, Amy, and I put our heads together briefly and decided it had to be allergies. "What was the common culprit?" we wondered. We settled on falling leaves. For the past few days off and on, depending on the whim of the wind, one would think we were in a sepia-colored snow storm, so great was the shower of beautiful autumn leaves all around us.

The Kleenex box in the room was a god-send. Amy and I made good use of it, coaxing the children to blow their noses, and then we would respond by wiping, wiping, wiping them. Little Bryan was especially uncomfortable. At one point he came up to me and said wearily, "Charles, my nose is soggy." I thought that must be the best description of that complaint I had ever heard.

I believe four-year-old Courtney's response to the early November, unexpected, heavy snowfall was a most thoughtful one, if not completely astute. "Mommy," she said, "I think God must have made an accident when He dumped all this snow 'cause it's only fall, and everyone knows it doesn't snow unless it's winter."

Sean McCartney's grandmother shared a delightful moment she had with him. The subject of their brief verbal exchange was chickenpox. Listen to these revealing few words of conversation they shared:

"Sean, are there any chickenpox at the day care?"

Sean's reply was immediate, and the tone of his voice was somewhat grave. "No, no, Grandma! There's no chicken poppin' at my school." He then gave her a "that's a dumb question" look.

Another time seven or eight children were at play. Mindy came up to me on her hands and knees and meowing like a cat. Everyone was impressed. I said, "Oh, this kitty-cat is really meowing. She must be hungry. Are you hungry?" Mindy nodded her assent. "Well," I said, "What shall we feed her?"

"Cat food! Cat food," was the response from the delighted children.

"What kind?" I asked.

"Meow Cat Food," was the instant reply.

"Here, Kitty, come get your Meow Cat Food," I said, going through the motions of feeding her. Suddenly I was surrounded by many kitty-cats, meowing for their dinner, so in my desire to be democratic, I went around to each one. Soon all but Zachary were eating. He was on his fours, but the sound was not that of a cat. "Don't you want some Meow Cat Food?" I asked, tongue in cheek.

His prompt reply was sort of a surprise to me. "No, I don't want cat food. I'm Pokey the horse, and I want some horse radish." So I gave him some, of course.

I had been away on vacation from the center for about two weeks, and I returned on a Monday morning, refreshed and ready to work a full week. The kids greeted me warmly, and it seemed that the first half hour that day we spent with their spontaneous outpouring of things that had happened in their lives in my absence. As frequently happens, one child would speak, and a half dozen others, more or less, would be "standing in the wings," ready to get their two cents in. Terrell was most enthusiastic when he said, "Charles, I'm going to the four-year-old class today. I'm four."

I wanted to be enthusiastic, so my response was, "That's wonderful, Terrell. I'm so happy for you."

As he beamed and walked away Angie caught my attention with this comment, "I'm going to be four someday. My mommie is older than four." Then, holding up two fingers like Winston Churchill in London during World War II, she added, "She's two fours." I smiled my approval and the thought passed through my head, "Would that be eight, twenty-four, or forty-four? I wonder." I decided not to ask.

Jaclyn was bustling around and getting in the way of Lala, who was putting the cots down in place for the afternoon nap. The children had been asked to line up by the door so we could go down to the gym for lunch. Suddenly Jaclyn plopped herself down on her cot with a deep sigh. "Jaclyn," I said in an annoyed voice, "I thought I told you to line up. What are you doing?"

She looked up at me with disgust and said, "I need my butt on my bed!" Undaunted, I took her by the hand and led her to the line forming by the door.

It is a joyful experience, indeed, when a young child comes to you with a small part of God's creation in his hand and lets you know in the language of uninhibited innocence the effect this gift from God has on him.

A case in point—recently, the three-year-olds were frolicking in front of the church in a burst of sheer energy on a cool morning in June. There had been a heavy dew the night before, and it was still early, so there were dewdrops galore on the grass and wild flowers abounding in the grass. Several children came running up to me with yellow dandelions and buttercups and pink and lavender clover, which were protruding here and there in the grass. Their comments ran like this. "Charles, look!" or "Look what I found, Charles," or "These are for you, Charles."

When one child started there was a spontaneous outpouring from many others. To see the light in their eyes as they gazed at the flowers, and then presented them to me filled me with gentleness and love for them. And with each gift I tried to respond with the joy and love I felt for them at the sweetness of these gestures on their part.

Then Michael came up, clutching in his hand something I knew was "special" by the combined happy yet mischievous look on his face. "What have you there, Michael?" I asked.

Terrell was close at hand. His usual curiosity was getting the best of him again. Michael opened his hand, revealing the tiniest buttercup plant I have ever seen—with two tight buds and one other just opening up. I wanted to cry, I was so touched by the beautiful simplicity of Terrell's comment when he saw the flower for the first time. "Look," he said in awe, "He's waking up." I drew both boys to me and hugged them with great affection. That experience really made my day.

2   Random Incidents - Imaginative

The next three chapters do not exactly fit into the group "Picturesque Speech," so I am calling them "Random Incidents." I had originally planned to include all my "Random Incidents" in one chapter. However, there are so many of them, and they are so varied in nature, I decided that perhaps I needed to sort them out and categorize them into three chapters. Thus, here we go with the first of the three breakdowns. I hope you will enjoy reading them as much as I have enjoyed writing them down.

The following is a brief but perhaps profound conversation between Joey and myself:

Joey: "How come you don't want to read any more stories?"

Charles: "Because I'm too hoarse."

Joey: "What?"

Charles: "My throat is hoarse."

Joey: (After a brief spell) "Open your mouth. I want to see the horse. Is he going to come out?"

Jason had spent several hours with Cathy, one of his day care teachers, because of a mix-up in arrangements for picking him up. Several days later he began reminiscing with Cathy about their time together. Greatly impressed, Cathy said, "Jason, you've got a good memory."

Ashwini, who was taking it all in, exclaimed, "I have a good memory too!"

"Oh, you do, Ashwini," remarked Cathy. Then facetiously she added, "Where did you get it?"

Without any hesitation Ashwini said, very seriously, "Toys R Us!"

I was reading a book to the four-year-old group on the subject of "autumn." We were talking about ducks flying south in the fall. I asked, "Do you know why ducks fly south in the fall?"

Carol immediately replied, "Because they can't walk fast enough."

Another time we were on the blacktop and four bicyclists were enjoying themselves. When I joined the scene they promptly lined up for gasoline and goodies—Matin, Sunitha, Patti, and Michael. It was Sunitha's turn finally! "And what would you like, Sunitha?" I asked.

"I want some snake egg cookies," was her mischievous, prompt reply. This really made a big hit with the gang, much to Sunitha's delight. Everyday now when we play this game, one or more of the children wants some snake egg cookies!

We were sharing our summer weekend experiences. Joey suddenly said, "I went to the swimming pool, and I broke my leg when I jumped in the water."

Feigning surprise, I exclaimed, "You did! Do you have a cast on it?"

Joey responded, "No, Stephen just put a Band-Aid on it." Chalk up another one for good old Band-Aids!

We were outside, and summer storm clouds began to gather, so hurriedly we dropped everything and rushed inside. A moment later it began to rain. Angie, brand new to our center, spoke very little English but was nevertheless very curious about everything. She was looking out the window when the first drops of rain began to fall. Very excited and somewhat concerned as well, she hurried to my side, exclaiming, "Sky making pee-pee, sky making pee-pee!"

Two boys and one girl, outside under the trees in the rear of the parsonage adjacent to the church center, were searching for acorns or whatever else might be lying on the ground. I was browsing around myself, and I spotted a piece of bark from a pine tree shaped like the paper planes we occasionally make for the children. The three of them saw me pick it up. I tossed it in the air with the remark, "Here comes an airplane."

Curtis was the first to reach the tumbled "plane." "I got it. I got it," he said excitedly, "I'm going to take it home." Angie mumbled that she wanted one, too. Naturally, I obliged. Immediately all three began jumping up and down in glee, exclaiming, "I'm going to take this plane home!"

Somehow I became caught up in it, and I exclaimed, first to Curtis, then to Angie, and then to Zachary, "And I'm going to take you home."

Curtis responded with a big smile, "Oh, no, you're not!"

Angie mumbled something unintelligible.

Zachary paused, looked me straight in the eye, and then said, "No, no, you can't take me home! I'm not an airplane—I'm—I'm—a bike!"

Laughingly I said, "And what are you going to be tomorrow, Zachary?"

He started to prance around, waving his outstretched arms. "A bird, a bird," he replied, with a very serious look on his face.

11

Kevin was pantomiming. It appeared that he was taking something from the wall and bringing it to his mouth, then taking rather large bites out of it. Suddenly he was aware that I was watching him, and he seemed a bit embarrassed—but not for long. He hurried over to me and tossed something imaginary in my direction. "Here, have an apple. They're real tasty. But be sure to spit out the bones."

As he moved past me, I called after him, "Spit out the bones? Apples don't have bones."

After a brief pause and a reflective glance in my direction, he said, "These do. They're chicken apples!" And then he broke into a roguish grin.

Sometimes in the classroom I make pictures for the kids—very crude ones actually, but they seem to like them. Recently we seem to have gotten off on a Christmas tree kick. If I make a tree for one, they all want one, so it wasn't long before Jarrod, waiting patiently for his turn, asked me a special favor. "I want a mommy Christmas tree," he said.

Obliging him, I remarked as I began my work of art, "Oh, you want a mommy one, do you?"

"Yes," was the enthusiastic reply, "And a daddy one and a baby one, too."

"It figures," I thought. "After all, last week it was mommies and daddies and baby bunnies. What else? Or did he just want three trees so he could be two up on the others? I don't suppose I'll ever know.

Maxine, our director, was concluding the reading of one of the favorite stories to the children in the circle. Her words were about as follows, "And when the little red hen had made the bread, she saw the duck, the pig, and the goose looking in her window, and she said, "And now who will help me eat the bread?"

They all said, "We will, we will, we will."

Looking up from the book, Maxine asked the class, "And what do you suppose the little red hen said?"

The new little child volunteered, "Cluck, cluck, cluck."

While I was resting in the gym after nearly an hour of vigorous ball playing with the four-year-olds, Kimberley decided I needed to see a doctor—Kimberley, of course! Going along with the idea, I said, "Doctor, I don't feel well. I think I need a shot."

"What kind of shot do you need," she eagerly replied.

"One that will make me feel better, I guess."

Presently she gave me an imaginary shot in the arm. Reacting like a child sometimes does, I said, "Ouch—that hurts!"

"Here's a Band-Aid," she said, "It'll make you feel better." Then she proceeded to give me a shot in the leg (and a Band-Aid, of course) and one in the ear (accompanied with giggles and a Band-Aid). Then she said, "Stand up." Like a good patient I obeyed. With a mischievous look on her face she added, "Now, I'm going to give you one in your butt." After a slight pause, and with much ado, she said, "You don't get Band-Aids with a butt shot."

The girls in the four-year-old room were talking about the director's decision to retire. Brittany and Melissa were particularly opinionated. Brittany was saying, "Mrs. Holden should retire. She's got grey hair, and she's a grandmother."

Melissa responded, "Yeah, she's old."

Doris Harne was eavesdropping, and she felt she needed to comment. "Well, girls," she said, "I'm a grandmother. Maybe I should retire, too. What do you think?"

Melissa's response was immediate. "Oh, but you're not old. Your hair isn't grey." Brittany echoed Melissa's comment and added a vigorous, affirmative shake of her head.

The story has a postscript of sorts. It would seem that Brittany's curiosity needed some satisfaction. "Mrs. Harne," she asked, "How come you're a grandmother but your hair isn't grey?"

Exuberantly Doris replied, "Brittany, there are lots of grandmothers who don't have grey hair."

"I know," said Brittany, "But how come some grandmothers have grey hair and some don't? Why is that?"

"That's a secret, Brittany, and I can't tell you," answered Doris, stifling an urge to be amused.

Turning to Melissa, Brittany's response was a gloomy one. "Did you hear that, Melissa? She can't tell us her secret." Both girls walked away. It was obvious they were very disappointed.

We were having so much fun in front of the church—a favorite place to romp and play early in the morning before the heat of the summer day. Before I knew it, I was ensconced behind the counter at "McDonald's," and all the kids were lining up to get some of that famous fast food. Like I frequently do, this time I wasn't taking orders. I was just passing out whatever I felt they, in their imagination, would enjoy eating. And so I said things like: "A hot dog with mustard and a coke for Tyria;" "A hamburger with ketchup, french fries, and a coke for Angie," "A hamburger and chocolate milk-shake for Nathan," etc., rattling on, going down the line, handing the goodies to one child after another. The children in turn were beaming, popping the imaginary food into their mouths, slurping away on their Cokes and shakes.

Then I decided to try something different. Tiffany made her appearance with her hand held out and her face bright and smiling. Casually, as I had with all the others, I said, "A worm for Tiffany." She popped it into her mouth, and then suddenly she registered surprise. Running off I heard her saying, laughingly, "Charles gave me a worm, and I ate it!" The kids burst into loud screams and jumped up and down. Then they descended on me, en masse, registering righteous indignation but still laughing. Need I say Tiffany was in the lead?

It was drizzling when it was time to go out on the playground, so we ambled on up to the gym. Before long the room was buzzing with great activity. The little bikers were flying by, children were climbing on the slide, the floor was host to several balls being bounced or tossed about. I was involved with the kind of vigorous ball play in which I often get involved. Suddenly I realized that Michael had thrown a ball up on the shelf above the coat rack and the emergency battery-operated light. It was sitting there in a tantalizing way. Knowing this type of ball throwing was a "no-no," I waited to see what would happen. Sure enough Michael came over to me for help. The following is a gist of our conversation:
Michael: "Charles, my ball is on the shelf."
Charles: "I see. And how did it get up there, Michael?"
I began to walk with Michael toward the shelf. There was a real long pause, as Michael pondered the situation, but I saw an unmistakably angelic expression come over his face. Then with a voice to match his innocent appearance, he said, "It walked up there." It was clear to me that he thought that would be acceptable.
Not wishing to make too much of all this, I reached up and retrieved the ball, adding, "Michael, please see that it doesn't walk up there again, okay."
His response was predictable. "Okay." And away he ran with the ball under his arm.

That particular morning at snack time, we had as the main attraction, in small paper cups, dry cereal composed of Wheaties, raisins, round, sweetened discs with holes in them, and corn-flakes. Erica seemed preoccupied with playing with each piece of the cereal before she finally popped it in her mouth. The other children were being their own silly selves, tittering and chatting away. As I was pouring seconds of milk I noticed that Erica had four identically shaped, neat piles of cereal spread out on her paper napkin. She was working on the fifth. "What are you doing, Erica?" I said ever so softly so as to assure an honest answer.

Without batting an eye she said, "I'm making hamburgers. See!" I looked closely at the "hamburgers" and quickly discovered that each one consisted of two Wheaties with a raisin in between!

Jeremy, in an imaginary playtime in the gym one afternoon, was completely absorbed in the role of "Big Fox" to the extent he was going around on all fours, growling, and nipping at the other children, and I might add, me, too! "And who is Big Fox," I asked, trying to understand his activity and show my interest.

"He's a big fox who lives in a spooky house."

"What does Big Fox do, Jeremy," I wanted to know.

"Oh, he eats all the other animals," he answered. Then Jeremy growled menacingly, grabbed my arm, and ushered me to his spooky house, which was littered with the corpses of several animals, played to the hilt by a number of the other three-year-olds. I pretended to be shocked by the ghastly sight and beat a hasty retreat with Big Fox in hot pursuit.

One time during free play in the young three-year-old class, Kimberley and Heather were showing great, maternal attention as they played with their dolls. Kimberley interrupted the feeding of her "baby" by going to the sink in the Family Living Section of the room and picking up from the stove what appeared to be a large salt shaker. Heather was watching her as she resumed her seat. Kimberley began to go through the motions of shaking the imaginary contents of the shaker in her "baby's" face. "I'm giving the baby some pepper," she exclaimed happily.

Heather's look in Kimberley's direction was a mixture of authority and contempt as she said in a slow, low, measured tone, "Babies don't eat pepper. Babies don't like pepper." Then after a brief pause she added disgustedly, "Babies drink milk." She got up from her chair and went over to the doll bed for a blanket.

Oblivious to what was said, Kimberley continued shaking away in her "baby's" face.

I'm sure there's a lesson here, but I'm just as sure I don't really know what it is.

Some of the two-year-olds were sitting around one of the tables during free time one late afternoon. Likewise, a few of the children were puttering around the stove in the "Home Area." Presently one came over to the table with an imaginary birthday cake, announcing to the seated few that it was time for the cake. Spontaneously the children began to sing "Happy Birthday to You." Then they began to blow out the invisible candles. Though Bryan was on the floor building something with the blocks, true to his canny ability to somehow never miss a thing, he had something to say. Reprovingly he exclaimed, "No, don't blow it! You'll burn your tongue! Don't you know that?"

Of course, no one paid any attention to his wise advice. He wasn't very happy about that either.

The scene was familiar. It was late afternoon in the gym, and the younger threes were blowing off steam usually reserved for the playground. But the weather was chilly and wet—hence the gym was the alternative play area.

Several children were pedaling furiously around and around on the popular, small, yellow indoor bikes. Others were bouncing balls. Some were racing one another—back and forth, back and forth. Two boys were wrestling on the mat. Everyone was talking or yelling at once. In short, it was a typical time of frolic for the kids. This is probably what they do best!

And then it happened. Shawn and April inevitably collided as they were running pell-mell in the midst of the delightful chaos around them. Both children dropped to the floor. Both rubbed their heads in surprise. Shawn got up and took off. April, however, was rapidly working on a wailing session.

I quickly rushed over to April, scooped her up in my arms, and stumbled to the side and the sanctuary of a chair, all the time consoling her. But now she was crying. Anxious to distract her, I began this brief conversation with her on my lap.

"April, where did you get your beautiful hair?"

Instantly she stopped crying, and her face broke into a delightful grin. Coyly she remarked, "From the store."

"How much did you pay for it?" I asked.

Fondling her hair now, she replied, "Thirty-eight dollars."

"Really," I said in a surprised tone. "What store did you buy it in?" Immediately she responded, "Green's."

By now she had forgotten her bumped head, and she slipped down to the floor. Eagerly she rejoined the merry group as they continued their ever-changing, innovative, lively romp.

Amused and intrigued by this delightful exchange I had with April, I tried a variation a little later with Paschal, a handsome three-year-old with large, very dark eyes. When he stopped in front of my chair in the gym and looked up from his bike to say, "Hello," I was ready for my experiment. This is what happened.

"Paschal," I said, "let me see your eyes." I reached down and held his face in my hands, looking deeply into his eyes. He seemed a little somber, but he said nothing, so I continued. "Where did you get those eyes, Paschal?"

Ever so casually he answered, "From the store."

"How much did they cost?" I wanted to know.

His response was fabulous. "They're black."

Not letting him know how much this amused me, I said, "Really?" I paused and then added, "How much did you pay for them?" Paschal seemed puzzled. I decided on another tactic. "How many pennies did they cost?"

With a big smile he answered, "Three pennies." With that he started to move on, but not before I gave another look at his face. I thought to myself, "Those dark brown eyes almost seem black. Maybe they are." Then, as he became a part of the traffic problem on the gym floor, I had another thought. "Paschal paid three pennies for his eyes, and April paid $38.00 for her hair. That's quite a difference. Paschal surely got a bargain price. Must have been a sale.

We were in the gym. I was teasing the kids—one of my favorite pastimes. Bryan, on a yellow bike, ambled on up to the group to listen to the nonsensical chatter. I knew from the look on his face that he wanted to be embroiled in the situation also; so as soon as I could, I said to him, with an air of curiosity if not concern, "What's that on your shirt?" Bryan looked down at himself and just grinned. "Seriously, Bryan, what's that on your shirt? It looks like mustard to me." (Of course there wasn't anything on his shirt. I knew it, and he knew it.)

Bryan, still grinning, responded by saying, "It's not mustard."

In an argumentative tone I continued, "It is mustard." I looked very carefully at the imaginary spot then reiterated, "I'm sure it's mustard."

With his best grin yet, he said very, very carefully and emphatically, "It's not mustard, it's mayonnaise." Then he pedaled off in search of new adventures, leaving me to my next encounter with the jolly group already on stage.

My curiosity was getting the best of me, I must admit, as I moved through the maze—children on yellow bikes, children running to and fro, children tossing and bouncing colorful rubber balls. And then I was close to a small cluster of boys and girls who were seated and transfixed by the appearance of Michael stretched out on the floor of the gym, eyes closed, lying ever so still.

I knelt down beside him, and as I reached out to touch him I said anxiously, "Are you allright, Michael?"

He opened his eyes and said as a matter-of-fact, "Yes, I'm okay. I'm just dead."

The kids in the cluster nodded in affirmation, looking at me as if to say, "Couldn't you tell that? We all knew it."

Now, why didn't I know that? Somehow, somewhere my education has been neglected, were the thoughts that raced through my mind even as I turned and walked away.

One morning the older twos asked me for the doctor's kit which was on the shelf. Since Tabitha asked first, she got to choose the doctor's instrument she wanted. I wasn't surprised she chose the stethoscope. (No matter who is first, it is always the stethoscope that is picked.) It was assumed by all that I would be their patient, and soon I was surrounded by a bevy of busy, young doctors. There was no doubt, however, that Tabitha was in charge. Simultaneously, as she was listening to my heart, Danny was checking my blood pressure, Sheena was giving me shots—all over, I might add—and Ashley was pounding my knee cap with his doctor's mallet. Throughout all this I was attempting to react as was expected of a good patient.

But Tabitha was so rough. By now she had tested my back, arms, legs, hands, chest, stomach, and you name it with the stethoscope.

Then it happened. Tabitha removed the instrument from my person and began swinging it, hitting my arms and legs with the ear pieces. "Doctor," I protested loudly, "You're too rough. If you're not gentle, I am going to go to another doctor, and this will be my last time with you!"

"You better not, " she yelled. "That doctor is no good. His swimming pool is yucky!"

("Well, well," I thought, "Swimming pools in the medical profession must be status symbols. Out of the mouths of babes...?")

The imagination of little children is frequently remarkable and delightful. Here is a case in point. In the gym is a wooden, box-like platform which is used for climbing and jumping on a mat. Down below, the top is supported by four wooden poles which are spaced wide enough apart to allow three children—at the most four—to crawl in for a fun time. It's a very popular place, as you can imagine. All sorts of curious antics transpire within this area.

At this particular time apparently it was a cage in a zoo, and the children were making loud noises appropriate to their choice of animals. I decided to get into the act. "Oh, look at all the animals," I began. "What kind of animal are you?" I asked one boy.

"A lion," he replied with a ferocious growl.

To another I asked, "And what kind of animal are you?"

His rapid response was, "A bear." This was also followed by a mighty growl.

I spied Ryan, and said, "And you?"

With his delightful Irish-American drawl he said, "I'm a dra...gone." The dra...gone gave a real loud snarl. And then they all moved closer to the bars and became very ferocious, lashing out at me with their arms and hands in scratching gestures. The noise was deafening, and of course, I reacted accordingly with hands over my ears, my eyes suggesting great fear, at the same time beating a hasty retreat.

It was later in the afternoon, sometime after her mother and older sister usually came to pick her up, but they had not done so as yet. Alexis asked me a question which completely floored me. I had no idea where she was coming from. She said, "When is my mother going to be finished at the dentist so the tooth fairy can bring her a new car?"

Several of the children were outside enjoying the first warm day of spring. Typically fascinated by worms that recently surfaced and nameless bugs that were scurrying along a patch of sand in the otherwise green grass, Kevin called attention to a particular bug which he decided was a ladybug. His entourage pressed and worked their way in for a closer look. Suddenly Matthew said, very determinedly, "That's not a ladybug. That's a boy bug."

Kevin reiterated, "It is a ladybug."

When Matthew repeated that it was a boy bug, I asked him, "How do you know it's a boy bug?"

He looked up at me and said, "Because some bugs are. They can't all be ladies!"

Seeing this as a possible learning experience, I said, "That's logical." Then as simply and briefly as possible, I began to explain that all God's creatures have names, and this bug is named "Ladybug." But he was right; there are boy and girl ladybugs. He looked up at me, and I could tell this explanation wasn't helping at all.

I was sorry I was unable to clarify the situation. In short, I guess I blew it!

For some reason my arrival on the scene of which Dennard is a part, prompts him to call out to me and express his views—often about me. Therefore, I wasn't surprised when I came with Doris and my class to the gym for our morning snack and he "sounded off" in a loud voice with most of the other classes to hear. Here's the conversation that took place.

Dennard: "Charles, you have a hole in your hair!"

Charles: "Yes, I know.

Dennard: (a mischievous look on his face, his fellow classmates enraptured) "Charles...(I interrupted)"

Charles: "Dennard, I don't want to hear another word! (pause) Unless you can say something to me that is nice, I don't want to hear it!"

Dennard: (after a brief pause and smiling impishly) "Charles, I went to the zoo Saturday and saw an elephant. He reminds me of you."

Charles: "Hold it right there, Dennard! That's enough! Our conversation is over...for now!"

I mean, after all, do you blame me? Since I'm skinny, it could be only one other thing!

On the morning following the reception for the new pastor and his family, the gymnasium was still not back in order. As we came down for snack time the children bustled about asking questions about the different "look" of the gym. There was a yellow balloon with a colorful string attached nestled against the ceiling. A small group of children plus a couple of teachers were gathered under it. Nickey, from the younger three-year-old class, asked me, "Charles, how did the balloon get on the ceiling?"

I replied, "I don't know."

"Did someone put it there?" she wanted to know.

My comment was, "I guess so."

"Who?" she inquired.

"I don't know," I responded.

She thought a moment, and her face reflected a big smile Nickey, in a somewhat philosophical way, then said, "Well, this is a church. Maybe Jesus put it there." Her classmates responded affirmatively.

Frequently all of us are caught unawares by some of the remarks of the children. We wonder what prompts them, what in their young experiences precipitates the comments. By the tone of the voice of the child, it seems obvious he or she is concerned.

Today Kashala moved away from several boys who were engaged in borderline roughhousing. Their voices were beginning to rise, and Doris and I, independently, were marking our time before our intervention. Kashala, obviously disturbed, went up to Doris. Pointing to the boys she said, "He said a curse word."

Doris responded, "What did he say?"

Very hesitantly and softly, in almost a whisper, she answered, "He said 'blue.'"

Michael B. had been studying intently one of the new plastic creative toys, one with a face. Puzzled, he turned to me and said, "Who is it?"

"I don't know, Michael," I answered.

Wide-eyed, he ventured this remark, "It looks like a ghost."

"Really, Michael," I said, "How do you know? Did you ever see a ghost?"

Never losing his momentum he said. "Yes."

"Oh, is that so? Where, Michael?"

His reply almost made me lose my composure. "In my church. It was a holy ghost."

Today before the children arrived in our classroom, as was my custom on occasion, I unloaded some things I had brought from home. Included was a cardboard Quaker Oats carton, an empty minced onion jar, and an obsolete catalog loaded with colored pictures from a large commercial firm. I enjoyed placing the articles in strategic places around the room. It was fun to watch the children, on their own, find them. Later when the children started arriving, the "treasures" were quickly discovered. Subsequently Dennard brought me the minced onion jar and said in a voice filled with disgust, "There is yuck hiding in there. It doesn't smell good."

Bryan, grandson of Frances, one of our teachers, is pretty sharp in his thinking even at the beginning of the day. Here is a typical example of what I mean.

Early one morning as I walked into the room to gather up my brood, I heard Bryan cough. "Where did you get that cough, Bryan?" I asked.

Instantly he replied (with a straight face, I might add), "My grandpa found it on a shelf in "Home Living" (pointing to the shelf), "and he gave it to me."

In like manner I said, "I see. I see." The trace of a smile on Bryan's face told me once again that he was very proud of himself and thoroughly enjoying every second of his repartee.

"Okay, gang, it's clean up time," I called out hopefully. There was absolutely no response. If anything, more miscellaneous toys were spilling out from obvious and not so obvious places. The floor was a mess. The din was deafening.

Amy came to my aid. "Listen, you guys, clean up." But she too, was being ignored. Then—in a real loud voice—the magic words, "One...two...three." The noise began to abate somewhat. Toys, books, dolls, crayons and paper, and scissors began to be scooped up and returned to the right places. Jigsaw puzzles suddenly got put together and stacked on top of the book shelf. True—two or three children on the fringe were casually ignoring instructions and were blithely continuing their play.

Then Andy decided he needed to be a part of management, so he said to Jay, who was trying to bounce a plastic egg on the floor, "Egg—give me egg."

Jay's response was, "No."

Andy's voice began to rise. "Egg—egg—egg!"

Stubborn Jay replied, his voice also rising, "No!"

Then Andy pointed his finger at Jay and almost screamed "One...two...one...two!" There was still no indication that Jay would clean up also. So—Andy's punch line, loud and clear, was "One...two...five!"

The weather was too cold to go out that early morning, but the children were busy, busy, busy in a time of free play before we got ready to go to the gym and enjoy our morning snack. Dennard was walking around carrying a bulging woman's purse, his royal blue cap looking so elegant on his head. As he neared where I was sitting he opened his purse and pulled out an empty Cepacol plastic bottle. Unscrewing the cap, he said, "Open your mouth, Charles." I responded immediately. As he peered warily inside my mouth and made motions as though he was pouring medicine therein, he must have noticed the few silver fillings in my back teeth. Wide-eyed he exclaimed, "Oh, you have earrings in your teeth!" Then turning towards several children standing nearby, he shouted, "Charles has earrings in his teeth."

All the children dropped whatever they were doing and rushed over, saying, "Let me see! Let me see!" Of course I obliged as one by one they lined up or fought over who was to look first or who would be next.

We learned today that Raphael's brother, weighing seven pounds fourteen ounces, arrived safely. After hearing the good news and all of us responding in a happy, affirmative manner, Nebelia proceeded with the early morning routine.

"Let's show on our weather chart today's weather. It is very cloudy."

Jordan moved the cardboard arrow on the chart to "cloudy" as the children milled around her. But Dennard argued that it was "sunny," not cloudy, and he hurried over to the window to prove it. Raphael hurried with him. No doubt about it, it was cloudy! Excitedly, Raphael explained today's weather thusly, "The sun is taking a nap—just like my mother."

Little Stephen was determined that if he was going to learn English, then I ought to learn Spanish. One day we had this enlightened conversation in the gym after morning snack time.

Stephen: "Hasta mañana"
Charles: "Hasta mañana"
Stephen: "Hasta mañana"
Charles: "Hasta banana"
Stephen: "Hasta banana"
Charles: "Hasta apple"
Stephen: "Hasta apple"
Charles: "Hasta mañana"

He was all smiles during this and delighted in my introduction of fruit (English spellings) into our exchange.

I thought no more about this, and later when it was time to go home and his parents picked up Stephen, his mother said to him, "Aren't you going to say goodbye to Maria and Charles and Amy and..." She broke off as Stephen rushed over to hug and say farewell to us. First Maria spoke, "Hasta manana, Stephen."

Stephen, as he hugged her, said, "Hasta mañana." The same thing took place with Stephen and Amy and with Marita and Stephen. Then, still smiling, he hurried to his mother who picked him up.

"What about Charles?" she said.

He looked over to me. I got up and went to him and said, "Hasta manana, Stephen," as I kissed him.

His response was, "Hasta banana, Charles," whereupon all who heard broke out in laughter. But the happiest one was Stephen.

3 Random Incidents - Completely Unexpected

I suppose you might say that all the incidents I have reported are, in a sense, completely unexpected, but there is a fine line I have drawn between the descriptive words imaginative and unexpected. In the first instance the events presented, by and large, reflect the children's creative, on-the-spot activities or language. For the group in this chapter, however, the children are seen using words or expressions that I felt were unpredictable.

Perhaps you will be as surprised as I was at their responses to these situations. I hope so!

Do you suppose this little tale I'm about to tell could come under a heading—shall we say—"Post Christmas Reactions?" I'll let you be the judge.

It was a few days before New Year's and Kimberley, Tracie, Amanda, Heather, and one other child (I forgot who) joined the "twos" briefly just before closing time at the center. Almost immediately it was "borderline bedlam" in that room. The visitors who seldom were in our room just had to play with all the toys, games, blocks, the music box and xylophone, etc., and of course, argue over who was to have what and right now! I soon wished I had earplugs to shut out the din, especially that hackneyed phrase often spoken with great anger and frustration by little children: "It's mine—mine!" And then the outburst of tears and the squabbling that follows. It can really get to you!

So I did what every dedicated teacher would do under the circumstances. I exclaimed, very calmly (I think), "Boys and girls, Miss Amy and I want you to put the toys away and come sit on the rug. I'm going to tell you a story." I tried to remain calm, anxious to gain control of the situation. But it took a little while (maybe five minutes?) before I got my point across and things began to settle down. Amy, of course, was a big help. She always is.

Finally I was able to begin my version of "The Three Bears" (first heard in my home about 1925). By the time I arrived at a crucial point toward the end of the story, most of the children's attention was riveted on me. I felt in control. I then said, "And so the three bears looked into the baby bear's bed. Who do you suppose they found there?" Naturally the response to my question was mixed. It included dead silence from some, "I don't know" by two, one said, "Goldilocks," and one or two other comments which somehow seemed pale in importance to the one that really sent me! (And I thought this was a familiar story!) I can't remember who the child was, but one said, very seriously, "Baby Jesus." No one...but no one...thought that unusual except perhaps Amy and myself.

One time I was reading to the two and three-year-old children in their room as they sat in a semi-circle. I had before me a large picture book with illustrated pictures of animals in various settings. There was a picture of some bears—two coming toward a cave. I then read the question under the picture, "Where do bears live?" Amy's prompt reply to my question was, "In a bear room, of course!"

Amanda always greets me with unbelievable joy, running towards me, smiling, and calling, "Charles, Charles!" and jumping up and down until I reach down and give her a big bear hug and a kiss on the cheek. Then she continues joyfully giggling, thrusting her leg between my legs, grabbing my leg and holding on, or my hand, oblivious to other "me, toos'" who have joined the fracas and are performing similarly (though usually not quite so ecstatically). After she calms down, often at the urging of co-teachers, almost assuredly she'll refer to me as "Daddy," which really tickles me.

One day, though, she called me "Granddaddy." "Granddaddy," I said. "Don't you mean 'Daddy?'"

"No, Granddaddy." She was insistent.

"Well," I said, "How come you don't think of me as a daddy?"

She exploded in laughter and then said, "Oh, Charles, you're getting older, so you're a 'granddaddy!'" It was such a simple thing for her, I guess, that she seemed surprised I didn't already know about it or I hadn't figured it out.

Outside on the playground one beautiful April day, the two and young threes were in the sandbox or on the bikes and swings, or climbing on their wooden stand which had become, among other things, a house to be lived in. Several other children were running around, up and down the hill, back and forth, back and forth, yelling loudly.

Suddenly one of the children asked me to be the monster again. Obligingly, I stalked around, baring and gnashing my teeth, and uttering loud, guttural sounds. Several children reacted typically—screaming and running away but always returning for more.

Then one of them, "Dramatic Vicky," told me she had to go to the bathroom, so inside the center we went hand in hand. A moment or two later while Vicky was still in one of the stalls of the ladies' room, I came to the door of the room and growled vociferously. Almost immediately

Vicky called out in her delightful Spanish accent, "Knock it off, Charles!" and I did.

I was having some difficulty quieting down the four-year-olds so they could settle in for their daily nap. Finally I got their attention. Then I said, for the second time that day, that it made the teachers very unhappy when they gave their classes instructions and told them what to do and what not to do, and the classes didn't pay any attention to them. Ana spoke up, rather appropriately, I thought, when she said, "Like the Sunday School teachers reading First Corinthians and asking the children to be quiet?" There was no doubt in my mind—she had gotten the point! I wished some of the others had when shortly thereafter the loud jabbering began again.

One cannot emphasize too often that sometimes little children can really surprise, even shock you with their shifts in moods sometimes during a brief conversation. To illustrate my point let me recall one incident I experienced with three-year-old Andrew recently.

I had minor surgery on my nose a few days before. When I walked into the gym Andrew came rushing forward, all smiles, to greet me. The conversation between us went something like this:

Andrew: "Hi, Charles."

Charles: "Hi, Andrew. How are you today?"

Andrew: (very sweetly) "Fine." (pause) "How's your nose?"

Charles: "It's getting better, Andrew. Thank you for asking."

Andrew: (with a noticeable change in facial expression and tone of voice) "How about your fat head?" Then, with a burst of laughter, he ran off, leaving me dazed and speechless.

At lunchtime one day Rayma was explaining to the "littlest" Jeremy, why it was not a good thing for him to put his hand in the soup. A gist of that enlightening conversation, I feel, is worth presenting:

Rayma: "We don't put our hands in the bowls that have food in them."

Jeremy: "Why?"

Rayma: "Because our hands may have germs on them. The germs will get in the food. Then children will eat the food, and they might get sick. Now what's going to happen when we put our hands in the bowls of food?"

Jeremy: (hastily) "I won't eat any."

Rayma's look at that moment said it all! It was a perfect response to Jeremy's perfect response.

Once when I was substituting in the three-year-old room, we were in a circle experiencing a group-time discussion about farm animals and animals in general. As you might guess, this subject is a very popular one with children. It is a constant delight to me how their curiosity is aroused and that they make such interesting and sometimes completely unexpected comments. Today was a case in point.

The usually reticent Brock, in the middle of a discussion about horses, suddenly broke into a beautiful grin and said thoughtfully, "Bees give us honey. They must like us." Not in the least disturbed by Brock's obviously irrelevant comment—on the contrary—the children verbally agreed, or at least nodded their heads in approval.

I was delighted not only by Brock's spontaneous contribution but also by the affirmation of his peers. It was another moment for me to give thanks to God for the privilege of working in a day care—this day care, to be sure. I can't think of another place I'd rather work.

It was about ten minutes past five in the afternoon, and the size of the two-year-old class had dwindled down to six children who were busily engaged in "free play" before story time. Stacey's mother came in, and of course, Stacey hurried to her, and they hugged. Stacey was chatting about many things. Sean and Bryan were busy building blocks. Suddenly Stacey rushed over and knocked over the block pile. Her mother registered mild horror and scolded Stacey. Her response was simple enough, "But they're always knocked down. Someone needed to do it!"

Again on the playground, I was busily engaged in pushing the two tire swings, each occupied by three happy older two-year-olds. There was a small group of their associates on the ground, watching the fun and itching for their turn. Some of them were occasionally vocal with the usual wail, "My turn, my turn." As was often the case, I was entertaining the children, verbally and lapsed into a question to each of them, "What's your name?" Their instantaneous responses as I pointed to each child were, "Tracy." "Andrew." "Heather." "Bryan." "Jennifer." "Jonathan." "Brock." "Ayesha." "Butch." "Sean." When I got to Christina she looked at me, and in a very annoyed voice she said, "I already told you my name. Once is enough."

I have a beautiful T-shirt my sister-in-law brought back to me from a recent safari trip to Kenya. It has a magnificent elephant on the front. One morning when I was getting ready to go to the Child Care Center, I decided this was the morning I needed to wear my elephant T-shirt! In the back of my mind I envisioned lots of questions not only from the teachers but especially from the kids.

At seven o'clock I was there as the first children came. By nine-thirty most of the children were on hand. A couple of the teachers had commented on the shirt, but nary a single comment came from the children. To put it bluntly, I was deflated and very, very disappointed.

Suddenly Ana came bustling up to me about a half-hour after her arrival to call attention to her "shocking pink" tank top shirt. "Look, Charles," she said, rather coyly, "see my new tank top shirt?"

"Oh, yes, Ana. It's very nice," I responded, not too enthusiastically.

"My Daddy bought it for me," she continued.

Sighing affectedly, I said, "It's nice, but how come you didn't tell me something about my shirt?" I wasn't too successful in fighting off the urge to pout.

"Oh, she said, "who cares about a dumb, old, boy's shirt?" and walked away disgustedly. I guess you know how I rated that morning!

P.S. by the end of the day only three of the more than fifty children present had made any comment on my shirt! I really had them pegged wrongly!

Matin was on one of a small line of bicycles on the blacktop at the rear of the day care. I had been pressed into service as a gasoline distributor and a fast food operator. Matin wanted his tank filled, and then he proceeded to reel off a number of items he wanted to eat. "I'll have a hot dog with ketchup, a Coke, and some French fries." Then a long line of sweets was mentioned. I filled his order, and he pretended to be eating.

It was soon obvious that his mouth was full and food was running out the sides. "Anything else?" I asked. He kept on munching the imaginary food and alternating putting more into his mouth, but made no effort to move on so I could wait on the next impatient customer. "Anything else," I repeated louder this time. He scowled and made a gesture of removing food from his mouth. Again I said, "Anything else?"

Finally he blurted out, "You know I'm not supposed to talk with my mouth full." And then he took off, leaving the impression he was very disgusted with me.

My next customer in line was Tally. "And what would you like?" I asked.

Her prompt, very casual reply was, "I want a new car for my swimming pool."

She ignored my question, "Why do you want a car for your swimming pool?" It was as if she couldn't believe I'd ask such a stupid question. At least that's the way I read the expression on her face as she took off on her bicycle like an experienced racer.

One day in the four-year-olds' class, I had the privilege of reading and telling the Bible story about Jesus feeding the 5,000, as found in John 6:1-14. When I got to the part where Jesus asked His disciples if there was enough food to feed the multitude, I recalled that one of the disciples said there was little or no food—only five small loaves of bread and three small fish, belonging to a little boy. The class had been studying the beautiful picture illustrating the Biblical incident and was transformed into the mood of the story. At this point Nicole spoke out. She was perhaps sharing the thoughts of some of the others—I don't know. Her question asked in sweet innocence was, "Why doesn't He go to the Safeway for the food?"

Sometimes one of the children will give voice to an idea or an incident that seems completely disconnected with whatever else is being said. That, perhaps, makes it even more interesting and amusing. Take, for instance, what happened during snack time one morning recently.

The children were enjoying bagels with cream cheese and milk. The atmosphere at the table was pleasant, but building up to a typical exchange of three-year-old silly remarks. Suddenly Tyria changed the tone of the chatter with this remark, "Charles, Jeremey poured water on my dress." (I observed that she was wearing shorts and a lightweight, sleeveless blouse.)

"Jeremey poured water on your dress?" I exclaimed incredulously. "Don't you mean on your shorts, Tyria?"

"No," she answered. "He poured water on my dress."

Again I quickly noted that her clothes were dry. Jeremey was silent and looked in wonderment first in her direction then in mine. "Tyria," I said, a bit annoyed, "you don't have a dress on, and your shorts are dry."

"But he did it yesterday at lunch," she said ever so casually.

"Oh, I see, I see," I said. "And why are you telling me this now?"

With immediate response she said, "Well, I forgot to tell you yesterday. And besides, I think you have a need to know."

Lala told me about an amusing incident that took place during snack time in the four-year-olds' room where she was helping out in the absence of the assistant teacher. The orange juice had been poured for all the children, and they were engaged in stuffing themselves with cookies accompanied by their usual innocent but somewhat silly chatter. Suddenly one of the cups of juice was knocked over. Lala responded to the uproar that followed at the table and began mopping up. Before she had finished another cup was accidentally tipped over. This prompted her to exclaim, "What's the matter here today? How come all this juice is falling on the table?" There was a slight lull in the chit-chat, and several seemed to be groping for a response to Lala's question. Finally Matthew volunteered this thought, "Miss Lala, maybe it's just gravity." The table buzzed their approval to this "logical" reply.

Three-year-old Kristen has been very conscious of her health since her serious bout with chickenpox which left her with an enlarged spleen. At least three times a day she comes limping up to one of the teachers to announce that she doesn't feel good or this hurts or that itches or whatever. Her dad works at the Naval Hospital, and I gather there is much talk in the family about medical problems and cures or treatments for ailments.

One day Kristen came up scratching an already well-scratched insect bite. Looking at me in a very serious manner and with a grownuppish tone of voice she asked, "Charles, what would you recommend for bug bites?" I tell you, I was impressed!

We were in a group time one morning (the threes), seated in a circle on the rug. We had shared a Bible story and the singing of several songs together. I was the leader that day and was interrupted by a late parent who needed to ask a question of me. As I was returning to the circle, I was delighted to hear Jeremey singing "Jesus Loves Me." (He's inclined to be very bashful as a rule.) Carlos, seated next to him, appeared to be enraptured by Jeremey's solo. Jeremey's sweet voice was intoning the conclusion of the song, "Yes, Jesus loves me the Bible tells me so."

Then, with no obvious provocation, he promptly bopped Carlos on the head with his fist! Carlos' face changed from surprise to anger. Jeremey calmly got to his feet and moved away from the circle. I hurriedly intervened in what looked like a counterattack on the part of Carlos.

For the record, I never was able to get an explanation from Jeremey as to what prompted the assault on Carlos. But I remembered that on several occasions Carlos had seen fit to bop Jeremey under similar circumstances though never with "Jesus Loves Me" as background music!

"Excuses, excuses, excuses," as the saying goes. "There's nothing new under the sun" is another trite expression. To that one I submit there just might be! Take the case of three-year-old Brock.

Upon arising from his nap one afternoon—very tardily, I might add—I ushered him into the bathroom where he sleepily performed. When he was finished, I urged him to wash his hands. He showed no enthusiasm toward fulfilling my request, so I urged him some more, helping him to stand on the bench by the sink and rolling up his sleeves. As I turned the water on in the sink he protested, "But I already washed

my hands this morning when my grandma asked me to when I got up!"
Needless to say, I was not sympathetic. More urging following, and
finally he complied.

At the gym, Ashley had gotten to the large blue vehicle first. He
was propelling it around the room by manipulating the two wheels by
their handles. Ashley pulled up to Ryan and stopped abruptly. Ryan
interrupted with loud squawking that he wanted that bike and began
bopping Ashley's head with his fists. Now Ashley was squawking.
Dennard, all this time, had been an enraptured observer of the fracas.

Nebelia, hearing Ashley's cries, hurried over to the scene. Ryan
saw her out of the corner of his eye. Quickly he turned to Dennard and
loudly exclaimed to him, "Don't bop Ashley...that's not nice." About this
time, Nebelia arrived. She found Ashley crying, Dennard with his
mouth open and a bewildered expression on his face, and Ryan smiling
like an angel—the very picture of innocence.

After nap time, Stephen was asked by Nazima and Nebelia to go to
the bathroom. He refused. When Mrs. Anderson and I came into the
room and we were briefed by Nebelia on the comings and goings of the
children, including Stephen's stubbornness, I made the same request of
Stephen and got the same response. Mrs. Anderson tried all to no avail.

Not wishing to upset Stephen, we set him at the table for snacks.
Golf, who had taken in the teachers' pleading with Stephen, turned to
him and said very loudly, "Go to the bathroom!" Stephen got up from
his chair rather meekly and headed for the door. I accompanied him to
the bathroom where Stephen did what was expected.

We washed our hands and joined the rest at the table. All I could
think of was the question, "Peer pressure already?"

For days Jordan had been talking about her upcoming visit to the
zoo with her grandparents. The last thing she said as she made her
rounds before she went home on Friday evening was, "My grandma and
grandpa are taking me to the zoo tomorrow." We all registered the
proper encouraging responses.

When Jordan came in on Monday we expected an enthusiastic little
girl to give us a "rundown" on her Saturday outing, but there was
silence on her part. By nine-thirty in the morning she still had not volunteered anything on the subject. I decided it was time to bring matters to
the forefront, so I inquired about her trip to the zoo. Reluctantly she
said, "Oh, I didn't like it at all. It smelled terrible!" Then disgustedly she
added, "The animals were going to the bathroom all over the place." My
sympathetic, unregistered thought was, "Talk about bursting balloons!"

We were having the best time with our conga chain. I was giving the calls in a somewhat melodious way. "One—two—three—kick. One—two—three—kick." The enthused children were following my calls in a happy circle. Suddenly Derek got a bit demonstrative. One—two—three—kick. On the last word he kicked Deirdre.

Silently but quickly I yanked him from the conga chain and set him on the chair. The conga chain continued, much to Derek's annoyance. His face was reflecting a very dark scowl, but that didn't stop us. We danced on.

During snacktime the other day restless Dennard was visiting at Vickie's table, where he gradually calmed down. Soon he and Vickie were chatting together like old buddies. At one point Vickie said, "Dennard, I think you look a lot like your mother." Wide-eyed and obviously pleased with what she said, Dennard's reply was, "Yes, I know. I've got her forehead."

David was a bit upset with the new boy whose vocabulary contained a number of very choice curse words. Finally after one especially bad sentence, he turned to him and said emphatically, "You keep that up and you'll be going down there!" He was pointing to the ground in a compelling manner.

Rose, a teacher in the three-year-old class, shared the following with me while in the hallway: "Derek apparently couldn't remember my name, so he called me 'Miss Flower.' I was so excited because he was thinking by association—and so young!" I can appreciate that this was an exciting moment in her teaching experience.

It was the second week of a really terrible heatwave, and this day was especially bad. It had been overcast for many hours and the humidity and air quality left much to be desired. Out on the playground little Rory, aged four, said to the director, "This air is so heavy with rain!" A bit amazed, I thought, "Right on!"

It was about eight-fifteen in the morning, and Doris and I were getting the children settled as they arrived. About that time Gabrielle waltzed in with her mother, who said to me after we exchanged warm hellos, "Gabrielle talks about you a lot. She really adores you."

At this point Gabrielle, her face alive with the sweetest smile you could imagine, rushed over to me and slugged me right in the abdomen. Sucking in my breath, and with a twinkle in my eye, I turned to her mother and said, "That's adoration?" The embarrassed lady could only laugh nervously as she hurried over to reprimand her nonchalant daughter.

I was called into the day care early one morning. The first thing I learned was that there was to be a funeral service in the church in a little while. Further, the director would appreciate it very much if, as we moved from the classroom to the gym or vice versa, we would make a special effort to remain quiet and orderly out of respect for the family of the deceased. They were receiving guests in the sanctuary prior to the services, so each group of children was briefed on what was going on, and ample time was allowed for questions from the naturally curious children. Happily, for the most part they cooperated splendidly.

Sometime later the four-year-olds were lining up after their naps, preparing to go to the bathroom. They were a bit noisy—their usual pattern of behavior. Lala, one of the teachers, was trying to quiet them. To her surprise, Nicole suddenly volunteered her support by saying, her fingers to her lips, "Sh-sh-sh, the people are still dead!"

4 Random Incidents - Tenderness and Reaching Out

One of the rewards of working with young children is seeing and hearing them in situations where they express qualities of tenderness and reaching out to others. Their sincerity and concern reminds one that they are truly the hope of the world.

How wonderful it would be if their child-like, unselfish ways would remain with us as we mature instead of us becoming self-centered and cynical.

Here are a few incidents I will remember as treasures.

Most of us, I am sure, have experienced the fun of overhearing youngsters singing songs they have learned. Often times the words are a little different, perhaps even strange, from what we thought we taught. But of course, to the child these words are the ones he or she had learned, and there is nothing at all strange about them.

Here is a moment worth treasuring that I'd like to share with you, and it illustrates my observation. Jarrod was off by himself seated on his parked bike in a corner of the gym. I was running after a melon-sized, tan rubber ball, kicked in my direction by one of the children. As I passed by Jarrod, I noticed a look of wonderment on his face. Then I overheard him singing in his clear, beautiful, boy soprano voice, with so much expression:

"Old McDonald had a farm,
G.I., G.I. Joe."

I stopped briefly to hear more. It came quickly:
"And on that farm he had a cow,
G.I., G.I. Joe."

I wonder why I enjoyed this version so much more than the original. Perhaps it was because it was so refreshing. Yes...Yes...that was it.

Cory, a new member and friend in the beginner's class, is a lovable, very active little boy. The second day I suggested to his mother that he was a "Dynamite Dunn" if I ever saw one. She laughed out loud and agreed with me.

Today in the gym he dashed up to me on one of the yellow bikes, all smiles, and began his routine of pushing, pretending biting, leg pinching, and then—the coup de grace—roughly running his fingers along the top of my hand. Then he pedaled away, leaving me to survey the damage—a noticeable bleeding hand though the wound was not really deep.

In hot pursuit on foot, I caught up to him in his reckless exuberance and snatched him off his bike. Though it was hard to hold him, I finally made him look at my hand. As usual, he was surprised he had done any damage, and he expressed his sorrow, looking at me in the eye with an expression of contrition. I left him deposited on a small chair to ponder the situation.

As I sat down on the piano bench several children came by, saw my scratched hand, and wanted to know what had happened. I filled each of them in quickly. Pascal joined the group of sympathetic onlookers. When he realized what had happened he sat down on the bench next to me, hugged me, saying comfortingly, "Poor baby...poor baby," and then he added ever so sweetly, "Don't cry, Big Bird!"

Needless to say, I was overwhelmed, and I gave him a great big bear hug and a kiss on his forehead. Then I went back to Cory, and we talked some more before I let him get up to resume his play.

Highlights for today...

I had barely gotten across the threshold of our room when Danny rushed up to me, obviously in pain. Before I could ask him anything he said, "My turtle is dead. My doggie bited him, and he cried. We took him to the doctor, but he died." My bending down and giving him a big hug seemed to help some.

Then...

Gathering up some of the first buttercups of spring growing on the church lawn, Laurie climbed on my lap. She pressed some of the delicate flowers into my hand, and a brief conversation between us began.

Laurie: "You're a boy, aren't you, Charles."

Charles: "Yes, I am."

Laurie: (smiling broadly) "I bet you don't know why, do you?"

Charles: (very curious) "No...why?"

Laurie: "It was God's idea."

Charles: (with a hug) "You're so right, Laurie. That it was."

Jordan was trying to make some conversation at the snack table today, but she was obviously very curious, even anxious, also. She had learned earlier that Michael's mother had died, and it seemed hard for her to believe. Always polite, she asked Michael, "Excuse me, but why did your mommy die?"

Michael's unabashed response was, "I don't know. She just died." Then he smiled and looked at Jordan and said, "But Daddy says someday I'll meet her in heaven." A beautiful, serene look appeared on

Jordan's face. You could tell she was relieved, and I, for one, was glad for that.

We teachers also have moments of tenderness. Here is one incident to illustrate the point.

The children were enjoying their gym play. The weather was nasty outside, so several classes were in the room this early afternoon. There was much activity going on.

Beth, Judeon, Deidre, and Michael A. were throwing the large red rubber ball to each other. When I came by Beth threw the ball to me. Once in the game, I alternated bouncing the ball and tossing it...to Beth, to Judeon, to Michael, and then off to one side so the four children could run for it. Deidre was pretty slow, and as often as I threw the ball, even in her direction, one of the others caught it rather than Deidre.

I was pleased with Deidre's patience—though secretly I wanted her to be involved—but it wasn't working out that way.

Then it happened. Deidre walked up to me, and with a big smile, she gave me her yellow tennis ball. I first rolled it to her. She caught it and rolled it back. Then I bounced it to her. She bounced it back to me. All the while Beth, Judeon, and Michael could care for less. After all, who would want to play with an old, yellow tennis ball when you could have a big, red rubber ball?

That left Deidre and myself and the yellow tennis ball. We played with it very well without any interference for about ten minutes when she tired of the sport and went over and sat down with another friend.

Of course, that was okay with me. Isn't that how a "good" teacher participates in a child's activity? I walked away, feeling that surely my halo was very obvious.

Kristina went over to comfort Anna, who was seated on a chair away from the group because she didn't feel well. She was crying very softly, and Kristina knelt down and put her arm around Anna and tried to cuddle her. I noticed she was leaning over Anna's face, so I said to Kristina, "Anna doesn't feel well. She has a little bit of a fever, and she says her tummy hurts. I think she might have a cold, so maybe you shouldn't breathe in her face...you might catch her cold."

Kristina gave Anna a friendly smile and then rose to her feet and came towards me. Looking up at me wistfully, she said very sweetly, "I had a cold once. I had a cold in Southern Virginia." I registered the proper interest as Kristina drifted back to the melancholic Anna.

In the usual confusion of play time in the gym, Ana came up to me, very excited. The following brief conversation transpired between us.

Ana: "Charles, Lafayette said a bad word."
Charles: "What did he say?"

Ana: "He said a bad word."

Charles: "I know...but what did he say?"

Ana: (very dramatically) "He said, 'No!'"

Charles: "Oh...well, thank you for telling me, Ana."

Ana waited a moment, and when she realized that was it, she ran off to become a part of the noise and confusion that was the modus operandi for the moment.

One day I came to work around the close of nap time and walked into the older three-year-old room. Patrick popped up from his cot and called my name. I asked him what he wanted. Noting that I had green socks, shirt, and pants, he said, "Charles, I don't like you in green."

"Oh," I replied, "what color do you like me in?"

"I think you need to wear blue. Blue is your color, not green. I don't like you in green." I thought, "I don't believe this."

Jeremy, that irrepressible two-and-a-half-year-old, had awakened from his nap and was going from one child to another, forcing himself on them in various ways—trying to tie their shoe laces or helping with their socks, whatever...but no matter how hard he tried, on every hand his efforts were repulsed, often angrily, by his little friends. Finally things just got to him, and he dissolved in tears. I moved over to him and getting down on my hands and knees, I attempted to let him know I cared. Then I began trying to tease him out of his despair. The following verbalization ensued along with the appropriate gestures on my behalf in his direction and withdrawal motions on his behalf.

Charles: "I think you need me to tweak your nose."

Jeremy: "No!" (tears still flowing)

Charles: "How about my pulling your ear?"

Jeremy: "No-o-o-!" (tears continuing)

Charles: "I know. You need your ear pinched."

Jeremy: "No...no."

Charles: "Shall I tug your hair?"

Jeremy: "No...no...no!" (no let up in tears)

Charles: (using my trump card) "How about a hug? Don't you need a hug?"

Jeremy: (moving quickly towards me and falling into my arms, his face alive with a beautiful smile) "Oh...well!" (And we hugged each other until his sobbing ceased...which was very soon.)

Erica seemed to be having a bad day. Several times she had come up to me to tell me that this boy or that girl had bumped into her or pushed her, or some such catastrophe had happened to her. I concluded that Erica was easily perturbed—at least today. Now we were in the gym, and all the children were very active on the bicycles, the slide, and with the large, soft, brightly colored rubber balls. The children were running and bouncing balls merrily, occasionally throwing them towards one another. Suddenly I heard the unmistakable wail of Erica, who was sitting on the floor. Hurrying over to her, I asked her what the matter was.

Between her loud sobs and the flow of tears, she said, "My eyes hurt. I need some ice from the kitchen to put on them."

Now on the floor myself and cradling her gently in my arms, I said, softly "Oh, I don't think so, Erica. They're not bleeding. Did you fall and bump your mouth?"

"No," was her response, "I don't think so."

Looking around quickly and trying to think of something to say to distract her or perhaps make her laugh, I asked as I spied salt and pepper shakers on one of the tables, "How about some salt and pepper?"

Surprisingly and between sniffs she said meekly, "Okay,"

I laughed a little, helped her to her feet, reached for a Kleenex for her nose, and said, "I know. How about some cold water?" We walked in the direction of the water fountain in the hall.

"I want cold water from the kitchen," she coaxed.

"Oh come on, Erica," I said. "The fountain is fine." She relented, and we both had a drink of cold water from the fountain. And afterwards? She was fine.

Yefim's mother told us today that when she was getting him ready for the day care and trying to get herself ready for work, he seemed more anxious than usual. He kept running to her and making it difficult for her to meet her deadlines. Finally she said in exasperation, "Yefim, what is wrong? Why do you keep pushing into me and getting in my way?"

His response was incredibly sweet. "But, Mommy, I need a friend, and you're my best friend." She said that she was overcome with guilt and just picked him up and held him very tightly. She knew she was his mommy, but she hadn't really understood until then that she was his friend, too...his best friend.

What a rewarding joy it is to see the children maturing! When the littlest ones come in, about age two or a bit older (and hopefully potty-trained), they are usually very self-centered and demanding. We all know this is "normal" for their age. As young as they are, to paraphrase the words of an old song, "They want what they want when they want it!" It's hard to get across to them the concept of waiting for their turn.

As an example, Rory, a very lively two-year-old, was subject to great temper tantrums and loud, long outbursts if he couldn't be one of the three on the tire swing. Time and time again we tried to reason with him to no avail and finally resorted to ignoring him. One day after he had been at the Center for several months, I was pushing three lovely girls on the swing. There were three others patiently waiting for their turn. Rory came up and said, almost in a wail, "I want a turn."

"Of course you do, Rory," I replied, "and you shall have it, but these girls are next." I pointed to the three on the ground waiting patiently.

It was a few minutes later when I said to the girls on the tire (all of whom had already gone through this stage that Rory was still working through), "It's time to get off now, so others can have their turns." The girls got off very nicely and hurried up the hill to the sandbox. The next three were helped onto the swing. I turned and smiled at Rory. He looked up to me with the sweetest expression on his face and said with a smile, "I'm waiting for my turn."

Overcome with joy, I gathered him up in my arms, gave him a big hug and a kiss, and said, "I'm very proud of you, Rory." Then I affirmed that he would be next. You know, I think he was proud, too.

It was late in the afternoon, and we were still in the gym. Several of the children were running around...among other things. Suddenly dear, little Kellie fell and bumped her mouth on the floor. When the teachers hurried to her side to comfort her and survey the damage done, she saw her mouth was bleeding. But worse she had knocked out one of her two top front teeth. She was surprisingly calm, and we put some ice cubes in a paper towel and asked her to hold it to her mouth. One of the ladies held her for a while, and pretty soon the bleeding stopped. We saved the tooth and later gave it to Kellie's mother. The next day when I came into the classroom at three o'clock, Kellie came up to me, and with a big smile she announced, "You know what? My tooth brought me money. I found it under my pillow this morning."

From the moment they were enrolled in the center, Carlos, aged three-and-a-half, and his sister, Monce, aged two, were very, very interested in all that transpired, but they were very, very quiet. We knew that this quietness on their part was likely due to their need to get acquainted and a hesitancy to speak English. But of course, there was never a doubt in our minds that they understood English.

One day after several months had gone by and Carlos was now much at home at the center, and when he had been speaking English for some time (when he felt the need to, that is), I decided on a bit of fun for us both.

"Carlos," I said, "do you know your name Carlos is the same as mine in English...Charles?"

Carlos' casual response was, "Yes, I **know** that!"

I gave him a big smile and said, "Okay, Charles." He really beamed at me, and I invited him to get on the rubber tire swing, so I could push three happy kids. Of course, he obliged, and a moment later three jolly tots were swinging away.

I hadn't seen Zachery for a long time, but one day several classes were in the gym together. When I saw Zachery I made a fuss over him, and he started talking while he was wrapping himself around one of the railings of the slide equipment. Suddenly he volunteered, ever so casually, "I've got a new sister, and she's not breaking my toys!" I learned then, from the day care director, that Zachery's sister Brook had arrived on the scene and was the ripe old age of ten days.

When Raphael arrived at the day care after a week's absence, he was well received by all of us. I wondered if his absence was because his mother was expecting the birth of a baby momentarily. I hugged him and told him how much we missed him. Then I asked if his baby sister was born yet. With great intensity, but paradoxically soft-spoken, this was his reply. "No, my baby sister is still sleeping in my mommy's belly, but she is going to come out soon...in February. When she does she will sweetly say to me, 'Hello, Raphael, how are you?'" His face was bright with anticipation as he hurried over to speak to one of the children.

A chain-like behavior pattern can easily be set in a classroom with little tots. Here's an example of what I mean. Ashwini, a pretty, little two-year-old from India, after some rough-housing with others in her group, came up to me and said wistfully, as she rubbed her posterior, "Charles, I fell off the bars, however and my bumps hurt." I bent down to comfort her with a few soft words and a big hug. My ministrations to her, however, did not go unnoticed by other children in the room. One by one they surrounded me, wailing ever so sweetly, "Charles, my bumps hurt, too." What could I do? Did I really have a choice? Of course not. I comforted each one, and as I did, at the same time I was secretly marvelling at these coincidences.

Sometimes children need that little extra attention...you know...especially if one is a younger brother or sister. As a teacher, one has to be on his/her toes and realize what is going on. Here's an example. Alexis came up to me on the playground with a half-smile and looking so nice in what appeared to be a new dress. Demurely she said to me, "Is my pretty dress pretty, Charles?"

"It's gorgeous, Alexis," I responded with a look of great admiration. She beamed the prettiest of smiles and ran off to join her playful companions.

I hadn't been to the day care for several days, and when I appeared on the playground one afternoon, Percy rushed up to me with the warmest of welcomes, a big smile wreathing his face. I bent down to hug him. Afterwards he said, "Charles, you smell so good. Where do you live?"

Doris has special, new hearing aids that fit into her ears and are almost imperceptible to one looking casually at her. One morning as she walked down the hall, she bent over to look at the new mural created by the four-year-olds—a summer scene. Alexis came by and spotted the hearing aid in one ear and quickly looked to see if there was one in the other ear. Upon verification, she exclaimed, "Oh, my God, what's the matter with your ears?" Doris explained that these were hearing aids and gave her a brief resume of the "whys" and "wherefores" and a demonstration of how they worked, etc. Much impressed and obviously deeply moved, Alexis hugged her, saying, "Miss Harne, I'm sorry. I love you, and I'll pray for you." Then she hurried off to rejoin her group.

5   On Stage - Actress Blaze

Chapters Five through Eight are perhaps unique in that each is about a particular child. I chose to devote individual chapter space to them because each, in his or her own way, is "special."

Blaze came across to myself and several of the other teachers as a born actress. It was not unusual for her to at times withdraw briefly from the crowd even though she was essentially a people person. At such times of withdrawal she seemed to be enraptured in thought. Soon she would return—seemingly on cue—with great dramatic intensity, and incidents such as portrayed in this chapter would result.

My one regret is that Blaze didn't stay too long with us. Most certainly there were other incidents not observed by the teachers that are left unrecorded!

On her first day in the Center Blaze called her mother on the play telephone in the Home Living Area of her classroom at least six times after her nap. From the gist of her remarks she seemed to be making sure that all was okay. She punctuated each time with the closing remark, "Don't forget to pick me up now!" The next time she talked on the phone she seemed to be running into difficulty. The conversation was longer and more animated. Suddenly I heard her say, "Well, if you're going to be **that** late, you'd better bring me a present!" Then she slammed the phone down and walked away in a huff, and an annoyed look crossed her face.

Blaze was intently watching Jason's mimicking of a TV hero as he strutted around, beating his chest with his bare hands and saying, "I'm a He-Man."

Not to be outdone, and in the tone of voice of a liberated woman, she said, "I'm not a He-Man. I'm a He-Woman," and she accentuated her remarks by beating on her chest.

It was one of those hard days—too long, too hot, and too noisy. As the afternoon dragged on I became more and more tired, and I was looking forward to going home. But we had only five minutes left of our gym time, and then maybe when we went back to our room we could do something less stressful and more restful, I thought to myself. I was wandering around among the children, trying patiently to calm them down, but some continued to be hyper. So when Blaze came bounding up to me all out of breath and asked if she could get the wagon out of the storage area, my response was predictable. Impatiently and firmly I snapped, "No, Blaze."

This really set her off. Pulling herself up straight, hands on her hips, her eyes searing with intensity, very indignantly she said, "I'm gonna tell my mommy, and she's gonna burn your buns!" And then characteristically she stomped off to be by herself.

Again the subject is Blaze and her completely unexpected and unpredictable remarks. Here I was, minding my own business, trying to cope with the day's pressures, hoping I'd be able to walk calmly out of the Center at the end of the day. What happened? Blaze bumped into me. (I really didn't see her coming.) With a big smile she spit out, "You know what? My brother has two babies in his tummy, but they're going to come out." And off she went, her face sporting a dreamy smile.

I guess you know Blaze's remarks are something else. I often wonder if they are spontaneous or if she thinks about them and stores them in her brain like a computer. I'll probably never know. Blaze's profound remark for today, completely out of the blue and unsolicited, was, "My mother always says, 'You can't get enough candy.'" Then she sped off on her blue bicycle, joining the others on the blacktop.

Blaze was still under the weather from a virus she had come down with a couple days before. She awakened from her nap scowling. Trying to make her smile, I said, "Blaze, where's your smile? Can't you smile for me?"

She shook her head "no" and said, "I left it home in the pocket of my jeans. I'll bring it tomorrow!" Then she got out of her bed lazily, stretched her arms, and Doris escorted her to the girls' bathroom so she could freshen up.

Blaze was in her usual "out in left field" frame of mind again. On the playground she idled up to Kimberly, looked her straight in the eye, and said, "I'm not going to hug you today. I'm a gorilla." Kimberly seemed nonplussed by this remark. Anyway, Blaze had her say, and so she left. Did I imagine she kind of staggered off the scene? Perhaps I overreacted...I don't know. I almost staggered off myself!

One afternoon I noticed that Blaze and Ryan were engaged in a lively conversation bordering, I thought, on an argument. Finally Blaze broke off the tête-a-tête by stomping angrily in my direction and tossing decidedly evil glances over her shoulder from time to time in Ryan's direction. As she grew closer to me I said, "What's the matter, Blaze?"

She responded in a testy manner, "Oh, Ryan hates love! He can't stand all that kissing!" Then she took off again, mumbling and grumbling to herself. I sighed, as I often do when Blaze shares one of her "profound" remarks.

6 Princess Tracie

You might ask, "Why 'Princess' Tracie?" Well, I guess because she is, to me at least, an engaging, lovable, complex, fascinating person. The term is one of endearment. These stories about her cover a period sometime in 1988 when she was only three-years-old to 1989. Already her vocabulary was well above average. She captured my attention because her inquisitiveness drew her, like a moth to a flame, into all sorts of situations. Here are a few based on my all too brief association with her.

Here is an incident to illustrate the competitiveness of little children and their attitude of wanting what they want when they want it!

One afternoon, close to the end of the day, my group, the younger twos, was able to combine with the older twos and all the threes into the day care lounge. Because of the hour, the number of children had dwindled, and this factor made it possible to combine the different age groups into one room.

The children love to go to the lounge because there are lots of different toys in large, open, plastic containers, many puzzles, and a great selection of books for them. Of course, the beautiful aquarium with its super collection of compatible tropical fish of many sizes, shapes, and variegated colors is always a mesmerizer for all of us. This day was no exception. No one was idle. Every one was immersed in some creative or thoughtful activity.

Several of the older twos were playing on the rug with brightly colored, interlocking plastic blocks. Tracie was working on a somewhat complicated jigsaw puzzle at one of the tables. Her eyes wandered around the room. She spied the children with the blocks. After a brief moment, preceded by a deep sigh and some mumbling under her breath, she arose from the table and hurried to the group with the plastic blocks, literally pushing herself into their midst. Inevitably borderline chaos began to develop, with whining, scolding, and scuffling taking over.

When one of the kids screamed as Tracie began to appropriate some of the blocks even as she dismantled others, I felt it was time for me to intervene. Still seated in a chair I said, "Tracie, leave those blocks alone. Those children are playing with them." She paid no attention to me but continued her obnoxious behavior, to the dismay of her companions, not to mention my chagrin. Finally I bolted from my chair and

45

moved towards her. In a menacing fashion I raised my voice almost to a scream, "Tracie!" Reluctant to cease what she was doing, she looked at me with a dark scowl and continued. By now I was right next to her. She yelled at me, "But I'm a big girl now. I can do what I want!"

That did it. I promptly lifted her up and out of the situation and set her on a chair as her tears and wails began in earnest. Regaining my composure somewhat, I said in a calmer tone, "Tracie, if you're such a big girl, you need to remember that you have to wait for your turn." But those words weren't much help. Her crying continued unabated until I placed a new book at her feet. Pretending to ignore this gesture, she brushed it aside with a sharp, "No!" But very soon afterwards she stopped crying and picked up the book. Soon she was completely absorbed with her newfound "toy"—much to my relief.

Tracie was apparently quite serious when she announced to me that she thought we ought to get married. "Don't you think we're rushing things, Tracie?" I said. "Why don't we just be good friends?"

"Nope," was her immediate response. "We need to get married."
"But I'm already married," I protested. I thought that would be the end of it.

Instead, unabashedly she said, "Oh, you mean the lady who talked to us over the fence one day?" "Yes, Tracie, that's the one. That's my wife." I feigned much seriousness.

"Oh," she rambled on, "she's really just your mother. Every one knows that."

Obviously I wasn't making much headway. Finally in desperation I tried another approach. (Actually, I was enjoying the conversation immensely.) "I've got a better idea."

Tracie interrupted, "What, Charles?"

With great enthusiasm I urged, "Let's go on a rocket trip to the moon, okay?"

"Okay," she said matter of factly, "as long as it's our honeymoon."

She seemed most determined and urged us to take immediate action. I had run out of ideas. But then it was time to leave the gym, and when Maria, her teacher, announced that fact with raised voice and some hand-clapping, Tracie joined the others lining up, and away they went back to their classroom. Naturally, I breathed a sigh of relief and thought about our class "lining up" in a few minutes so that we could make ready for the "older" threes who would be appearing at the gym door, ready to create their own brand of pandemonium and fantasy.

Accidents happen all too often when a group of children are involved in active play. And they can impose pain on all involved, not just the ones who are physically hurt. A case in point...

Three-year-old Andrew, a handsome lad with blond hair and beautiful, expressive brown eyes, was his usual wild self at the gym one afternoon. He was rumbling and tumbling all around—and not only on the mat where he should have been.

The accident was sudden though perhaps not completely unexpected. Sometimes a teacher begins to feel anxious about a developing situation. It's almost like a sixth sense. No doubt parents and baby sitters have experienced this feeling too. As a parent I know I have.

Andrew was crawling through the popular barrel which is suspended by a wooden frame a few inches from the floor. His entourage of like-minded, seemingly adoring boys and girls were following their buoyant leader through these lively paces. Suddenly Andrew decided he needed to be alone in the barrel, and strangely, he got his way. I was watching from a distance, and I noticed the barrel was tipping forward. I barely had a chance to run over when Andrew came tumbling out. His immediate outcry indicated he was really hurt. Three or four other children now were going through the container and quickly spilled out on top of Andrew. Amy joined me as I sought to disengage the kids from the pile. Immediately thereafter we discovered to our dismay that there was a deep gash below one of Andrew's fingernails, and the blood was flowing...I mean flowing! (Later we decided that the barrel, around the metal edging, had pinned his finger to the floor.)

By this time most of the two and three-year-olds in the room were on the scene, in general very upset, especially with the sight of blood. I scooped Andrew up in my arms just as Phylis was coming through the gym door with a child she had taken to the rest room a brief moment before. As I was coming toward her with the screaming, bleeding, frightened little boy, followed by his equally frightened and curious peers, Phylis sensed what to do. She took Andrew from my arms and proceeded to hurry out the door. Amy gave her a wet paper towel which she pressed to the wound. Phylis, at the same time, was trying to comfort the screaming Andrew.

Amy decided Phylis might need her help, so she, with my approval, followed her. This left me to clean up the blood and to try to comfort the unhappy children, some of whom were crying, all of whom were expressing dismay at the small pool of blood by the barrel and the trail of blood across the gym and out the door.

I suggested firmly but lovingly that all the children sit down on the mat adjacent to the barrel while I wiped up the blood. Then followed the inevitable questions and comments. "What happened?" "Look at all the blood!" "Is Andrew okay?" And of course, "Why?" to each of my responses. I attempted to answer the questions as I worked on the messy floor at top speed, a bundle of paper towels at my fingertips.

I was especially touched by Tracie's expressions of concern. Tearfully she said, "My little friend Andrew is bleeding. Why is he bleeding? I don't want him to be bleeding. He's my friend."

I responded as softly and calmly as I could. "That's okay; he's going to be allright. Don't worry, Tracie. Miss Phylis will take care of him." All this as I continued cleaning up.

When the floor was cleaned and hastily washed with cold water and wiped with more of the paper towels, I gathered the still crying Tracie into my arms and sat down on the mat with the other children. Gradually, thanks to my continued ministrations and to God's help, Tracie quieted down. Almost immediately the others followed suit.

Shortly thereafter Amy returned with the good news that the director had come down to help Phylis, and that they had an ice compress on Andrew's hand. His grandmother was on the way. But best of all, she assured us that Andrew was allright and that he was being very brave.

By now the group was calm, and shortly they returned to their play. I put the barrel back on the wooden support, but it didn't seem to have any appeal to the children the rest of the time they were in the gym. I wasn't at all surprised by their disinterest in it.

Do you remember that great film of the late 1930's, "Ninotchka?" It was about a dedicated Russian Commissar, Greta Garbo, and her meeting the sophisticated Parisian man-about-town, Melvin Douglas. You may recall that wonderful scene where the reserved Greta is beginning to melt a little under the influence of the suave Melvin. She subsequently visits an exclusive Parisian shop and winds up seated before a large, vanity-like mirror gazing at herself and contemplating the purchase of an extraordinary chapeau which is perched, strikingly, on her head. The camera stops for a brief moment as you survey the expression on Greta's face. It is indescribably enchanting.

"What has this to do with the day care?" you may ask yourself. Well, let me tell you. When I spied Tracie on the playground that unexpectedly warm day in late March, she was draped over one of the automobile tires embedded in the ground. Her pose immediately reminded me of that moment in "Ninotchka" which I described above. Of course, Tracie wasn't wearing a hat, but her intense, contemplative stare seemed to be the same as Greta's!

With this as my cue, I rose to the occasion. Rushing over to Tracie, in my best dramatic manner I exclaimed glowingly, "Who is this gorgeous creature?"

She fluttered her eyelashes seductively and responded, "Cinderella."

I bowed and scraped a little and said, "I'm delighted to meet you. And where is your Prince Charming?"

She sighed and then replied, "He's gone to another day care." (I recalled that Andrew had enrolled a few days before in a day care closer to his home. No doubt he was her Prince Charming.)

"Well, I hope you'll see him soon, my dear," I said.

"Me, too," she replied sadly. Then, disengaging herself from her pose, Cinderella became Tracie once more and rushed off to some new pursuit.

The next day and for several days thereafter, when Tracie spotted me she hurried over to me and said something like this, "Will you do the gorgeous creature routine with me, Charles?" (Yes, she did use the word "routine.")

"Sure," was always my response. She was insistent that she be in the same place, draped over that automobile tire. And the "routine" would begin. If inclement weather forced the locale for the drama to be switched to the gym, then she draped herself appropriately either over a chair or the bench adjacent to the slide. But it had to be the same dialogue, which she monitored very carefully.

One day I mentioned, "I'm sorry...I'm sure you miss him," (referring to the handsome Andrew).

Tracie responded, "Yes, I do." Then with a flirtatious smile she added, "Well, he and I may get a divorce. You never know."

Several days after these performances I met Tracie's mother in the hall outside Tracie's classroom. After work she had come to pick up her daughter. She greeted me, "Tracie is so enthusiastic about the Cinderella act you two go through."

I laughed and said, "It's been fun."

She added, "She seems to get a big kick out of it. But like everything else, it will probably lose its appeal one day."

"Yes," I thought, "This, too, shall pass."

Now, weeks later, our classes no longer meet at play time. Tracie has moved up to the older threes, and they meet by themselves. I wonder sometimes, "Has it passed?" Such a profound speculation; don't you agree?

You can count on Tracie to be imaginative by way of reacting to a particular situation. A case in point occurred recently.

Because it was too cold to go out, we were preparing for the alternative visit to the gym. On such occasions we sometimes try to encourage the children to be quiet in the hallways by choosing a leader, and the others line up behind the one chosen. Ideally, then we can proceed to our destination with a minimum of noise and confusion. It is intended for them to learn to follow directions.

I picked Tracie for the leader that afternoon, and by the time we arrived at the gym, she proved to be such a wise choice that I felt praise for her efforts was warranted. "Tracie," I said, "you are a good leader. You did a good job." She beamed at my approval, and those unusually remarkable, soft, expressive eyes were a delight to behold.

However, on the return trip the story took a different turn. Our leader Tracie was "full of herself," as the saying goes. She was singing loudly and swaying and jumping up and down the stairs, completely oblivious to my occasional loud attempts to get her to behave. Of course, the rest of the children were performing in like manner. Finally, in exasperation I said sharply, "Tracie, you're fired!"

Well, that did it! Tracie stopped short, put her hands on her hips, stomped her feet a few times, and then rising on her toes and looking at me with blazing eyes, she said to me with obvious contempt, "Nobody fires Tracie!" With that she deliberately marched forward toward the classroom, the children following her passively.

I know it's trite to say, but I do believe you could hear a pin drop, so quiet was the aftermath of our verbal exchange. No one needed to tell me the obvious—the final word on **that** subject had been spoken.

The fall days were growing shorter, and we were taking advantage of the glorious afternoons by spending time on the playground at the center. On one of these occasions, the children were running through the leaves, kicking them up into the air with great glee. The contagion of mirth that this pattern of behavior spread was suddenly punctuated by an outcry from three-year-old Tracie. The curious children ran to her side and some came running my way afterwards. By now Tracie was crying—almost wailing. As I hurried over to be of assistance, I thought of several things that might have prompted her tears: a bee sting (God forbid!); she had fallen and hurt herself; one of the children had been hurtful (either verbally or physically) to her. "What?" I wondered. Finally at her side, I said anxiously, "Tracie, what's the matter?" In her anguish she was jumping up and down, pointing to the ground, and her remarks were incoherent.

I looked down and discovered a dead pigeon, ravaged by swarms of ants, at her feet. Holding her in my arms, there didn't seem to be anything I could say to comfort her. Finally when I suggested a proper burial for the unfortunate creature, she was ready for an explanation of what probably happened...the pigeon fell to his death, or an animal (a cat, perhaps) had caught it, whatever. This prompted many questions both on her part and the other childrens, who by now had milled around. It was time for a "lesson to be learned," and I secretly prayed that God would help me to say the right words so that the children would be comforted.

The big questions, as always, seemed to begin with "Why?" "Why did the pigeon die?"

My answer: "I don't really know; I can only guess. Perhaps he was sick or something and fell off the roof of the building, or perhaps he was walking on the ground, and he was not as careful as he should have been, and a cat or dog jumped on him, or maybe somebody shot him with a BB gun...I really don't know."

"Why did a cat or dog jump on him and hurt him?"

My answer: "Sometimes a cat or dog or some other animal will jump and grab a bird. That's the way they are."

"Why?"

A pause as I meditated briefly and then my answer: "I don't know."

"Why should someone shoot a pigeon?"

My answer: "Well, some people like to be hunters, and they shoot birds or animals."

"But why?"

My answer: "They just do...maybe you've seen this happen in the movies or on TV". Some heads shook in the affirmative, but still the wonder and sadness was in their eyes.

My calm, measured remarks were understandably interrupted from time to time by my need to say to the children that they were not to touch the bird or move it around with twigs from the large oak tree nearby, etc. Gradually God helped me to bring order out of the mixture of despair and sadness, and after I dug a hole and buried the unfortunate pigeon, the group quietly moved away to pursue other avenues of interest.

I was aware again of the sensitiveness and the beauty of the loving, caring children. It had been a sad time for us all but a memorable one. I needed to be reminded that little children are truly remarkable creations of God, and that I was where He had need of me that afternoon. It is times like this that I am affirmed in my ministry to the children at the Center. I'm glad for the privilege of working there.

7   Our Gal Chrissy...Our Guy Butch

There is a simple explanation for my combining incidents about two people not even involved in the same stories. The fact is, there is very little information about Butch, and even less for Chrissy, to warrant each being the subject of a chapter. So..."Why not combine the two chapters into one?" I asked myself. The answer came loud and clear...why not!

My fascination with Chrissy stemmed from her unusual handling of the English language. Not only did she have a strange twang when she spoke, but her choice of words captured the attention of myself and others.

Butch's charm was his apparent love of life. He seemed to approach each day with complete immersion into everything going on and with those about him.

Why did I choose to record Chrissy's comments for posterity first? Ladies first is the right way to go! I hope you enjoy Chrissy's and Butch's stories.

One wonders sometimes what unusual thoughts go around in the minds of young children. For instance, how do they arrive at some of their word associations? One of the delights in conversing with them is the unexpected comments they make in response to what you think are clear-cut thoughts that you've expressed to them. As an example, consider this little vignette that happened recently.

Chrissy and Katie were coloring a picture of a man—a preacher behind a pulpit. Katie was trying very hard to keep within the line of the drawing, but Chrissy was very sloppy with her use of the crayons, using many colors, and with no obvious attempt to keep within the lines of the drawing. Presently this prompted the following conversation:

Charles: "Chrissy, please try to be more careful and not so sloppy."

Chrissy: "I'm not being sloppy. What do you think I am, anyway, a wizard?"

Charles: "What's a wizard?"

Chrissy: "Oh, one of those things that crawls on the ground."

Charles: "You mean a lizard, don't you?"

Chrissy: "No, I said a wizard."

Charles: "I think you mean a lizard, Chrissy."

Chrissy: (pouting) "I do not. You can call it a **lizard** if you want, but I'm calling it a **wizard**. It's a **wizard**." (And she furiously grabbed a different crayon and rubbed it almost violently on the paper.)

Lizard or wizard—what do either have to do with sloppy coloring? I tried to push the subject further but to no avail. It was obvious that Chrissy couldn't (or wouldn't) comprehend why I didn't get the connection, and she wasn't about to explain to me, an adult, something she thought was so obvious.

One day when I came into the room of the two-year-olds and interacted with the kids as we first saw one another, they came running to me with big smiles and open arms. Chrissy finally got my attention. "Mister Charles," she said, "I know how to fall. I've been practicing."

"Oh, how is that, Chrissy," I said.

"I fall on my butt!"

Never dismayed at what they might say, I responded casually, "And why do you fall on your butt, may I ask?"

Her response was instantaneous and very much to the point. "Because when you fall on your butt it doesn't hurt too much...with all that padding."

"I see...I see," I said.

Chrissy sometimes gets her words in a sentence mixed up or at least out of order, but there is no problem, as a rule, understanding her. Nevertheless, her sentences sometimes make me smile. Once she said to me, "I have two dogs. They always like on everybody's laps to climb."

On one of those glorious April days Chrissy ambled up to me and flashed her coquettish smile. "Hi, Chrissy," I said, "how are you?"

"Foine," was her response. "Did you have a nice **trop**?" "Trop," I said questioningly. "What's a **trop**?"

Faintly annoyed she said, "**Trop...trop**. You know, you get in a car and take off!"

"Oh, you mean **trip**," I replied.

"Yes, **trop**, that's what I said...**trop**." Then she filled me in on her "trop" to see her mommy and poppy, her very own mommy's daddy and mommy. Then a stream of words flowed rapidly—all about her visit. The words at times were not too intelligible, spoken in her peculiar English pronunciation, but I gather from the tone of her voice and her fascinating expression, that all was indeed well with those grandparents and the time she spent with them. It was a good "trop," if you know what I mean.

The initial entry of Butch into our day care produced a new scenario...long bouts of loud crying. Butch was three though very small of stature. He apparently had not been exposed to a group situation before. Rather, he had a sitter who seemed to have catered to his every whim. He cried constantly and clung fervently to his little teddy bear. Maria, his teacher, was worn out by his continuous wailing. After about two weeks of this Maria, a minister's wife, in desperation prayed to God that Butch would stop crying. Otherwise, she didn't know what she would do. Her prayers were answered for the next day Butch quieted down and quickly "settled in." All of us were relieved. Surely it was a small miracle.

Shortly after "Butchie's" adjustment to the routine of the Day Care, to our delight he became one of our happiest, though somewhat mischievous, well-adjusted youngsters. Consequently, he very quickly endeared himself to the teachers and many of the children. At first we had some difficulty getting him to obey the rules but realized a language problem was the culprit. Then we noticed he hung on every word of his teachers.

Of Thai background and striving to be bilingual, a recent incident showed his determination to succeed. His mother, while picking him up in the evenings, usually spoke to him in the Thai language, and he would obediently respond. One evening, however, as his mother sought to converse with him, he unexpectedly expressed his displeasure. His sunny smile turned to a surly pout. As she continued to talk, he finally interrupted her, and in a loud, annoyed voice he exclaimed, "Butch speak English! Butch speak English!" Happily, she quickly got the point and proceeded to oblige, much to Butch's satisfaction.

It was certainly a good time of day, lunch, with a menu most children and teachers alike appreciated, main course, spaghetti with meatballs. It's always amazing how good the children are and how quiet it becomes when the menu meets with their approval.

I looked around at the tables and smiled as I saw everyone eating with great relish. (Excuse the pun!) However, one child at our table, four-year-old Katie, was making so much noise slurping her spaghetti that Butch, sitting opposite her, was quite distracted. Soon he stopped eating and glowered at her. Katie finally noticed, and grinning, she said, "Why aren't you eating?"

Butch replied with obvious disgust, "Yuck!"

Laughingly, Katie, slurping away, asked, "What's the matter?"

Butch let her have it. "You're like a chicken eating worms!" Katie giggled between slurps, but kept right on eating. Butch sighed deeply, and put his fingers in his ears. Then when he realized she was going to continue eating noisily in spite of what he had said, Butch began to eat again.

The noise stopped long enough for Katie to ask, "May I have some more spaghetti, please?" Then she resumed her slurping, much to Butch's obvious disgust.

Out on the playground one sunny afternoon some of the younger children were rolling down the hill. Phyllis, one of the teachers, perhaps in a playful mood, crouched on the grass at the bottom. Presently several tots rolled on top of her in a great frenzy. Butch was the last to do so and the first to get up and survey the chaos of the moment. The sight prompted this astute comment on his part, "Oh, oh...better get MAAKO!"

There are several dolls with special appeal to the children in one classroom. Often boys that age are just as interested in playing with them as are the girls. Butch is no exception, but sometimes he gets in the act, so to speak, tardily and ends up with little choice. One day in particular he was observed talking to the old man doll. Some of what he was saying was not too clear, but one phrase he said often enough for it to be very plain, "Ugly baby. Ugly baby."

There was little love expressed in the chatter. Rather it was more like, "Why do I have to play with this doll? Why can't I have a **pretty** one, too?"

Wow! They express those feelings that young in life? It's humorous, to be sure, but kind of scary, too!

8   Righteous Indignation

An attribute of most children is that they have a propensity to run out of patience with their peers and others, especially adults, when we least expect them to do so. Again our surprise can be a delight if we don't run out of patience ourselves.

Here are a few tales about these little ones that you might call "moments of righteous indignation."

At lunch one day we were standing, hands linked together, awaiting the blessing from the director before we sat down to eat. After the prayer I squeezed the hand of the child to my right and the one to my left, as I do automatically at such times. Genese scowled at me saying, "You squeezed my hand! I'm going to tell my mother."

I said, "That's okay with me. You do that." A moment later she was fussing with the child on her right. I told her to stop fussing.

Her annoyed response was, "I'm going to tell my mother on you." Later she asked for a fourth slice of melon. I explained that there wasn't enough, that some children only had two, etc. Furiously she exploded, "I'm going to tell my mother on you."

Exasperated at last, I said very pointedly, "Go ahead. I don't care. In fact, you can call President Reagan on the phone and tell him, too, for all I care."

She really scowled then and after a brief pause blurted out, "I might just do that! And then you'll see."

On Friday while the whole day care was participating in the chapel service in the Music Room of the church, our director, Rayma Hyatt, looked around at the group and saw a sea of glum-looking faces. This prompted her to remark, "Everyone looks so sad and grumpy. How come? You're supposed to be happy. What kind of a look is that, anyway?"

Angie, probably feeling she was spokesperson for the school, replied loudly, "That's a Dwayne look!"

We all smiled and some giggled as Angie riveted her attention on Dwayne. He had previously done something that prompted him to be fussed at by his teacher. No wonder there was a look of chagrin on his face as he sat facing the group.

so you can understand the great deal of animated interest it created. Maxine, the director at that time, thought she needed to discourage this kind of activity. "Shawn," she said, "you really shouldn't have brought in that worm. Why...he might die."

Timmy reflected his disgust with that comment by saying, "Well, he's **not going to eat it,** for goodness sake!"

The very little, very young, and very pretty girl was on the commode. I was outside the bathroom, waiting to be of assistance. Suddenly she called out very sweetly, "Charles, wipe my butt."

I wasn't sure I heard her correctly, so I asked her, "What did you say?"

Her quick, somewhat annoyed reply was, "Wipe my butt! I haven't got all day!"

Jamie was "all ears" as he watched me firmly inform Justin that he had to stop running inside the room and adding to the great confusion at the end of a long, hot, noisy afternoon. I very meticulously spelled out why Justin couldn't run, how such conduct was only permitted in the gym or the playground, never in the classroom, how I was distressed that he persisted in this, how I was running out of ideas to correct this situation, etc. I punctuated my remark with the terse comment, "And if you don't stop this, I don't know what I will do!"

Jamie, wishing to be of some assistance I suspect, came up to me and indicated he needed to whisper to me. I bent down, and he put his mouth close to my ear. Then very seriously he said, "Call the police!"

As a postscript to the above incident, the next day a similar situation developed with, of all people, Jamie! Having been driven to exasperation, and probably to tease him a bit, I said, "If this doesn't work—my fussing with you—I may have to call the police."

He looked up at me and with great authority in his voice he replied, "I don't think I'd do that if I were you!"

Nephelth hurried over to the small phonograph on the table and started messing with the record and needle. This is a "no-no," as all the kids are aware. I called across to him that he should not touch the phonograph. He ignored my command. I called again a little louder and was still ignored, so I started across the room just as the unmistakable noise of the needle scratching across the record met my ears. Right on top of him now, and very indignant, I asked, "Nephelth, are you listening to me? PUT THAT NEEDLE DOWN!"

Still messing with the cartridge, he turned his head in my direction and looking up to my face, said very softly but firmly, "If you keep this up, I may have to tell my mother." In my mind I began to count to ten as I fought to regain my composure.

Trying to encourage a grumpy Jennifer, aroused from her afternoon nap, into a more cheerful frame of mind, as I opened the window blind I remarked on the sun streaming through the window. "Isn't the sun warm and friendly?" I said eagerly.

She scowled as she replied most emphatically, "No...the sun is out!" Taken aback by her bluntness and perception, I was at a loss for words.

Several girls were in the bathroom talking loudly and squealing. As I hurried out of my classroom the shrill noises were getting to me. With great authority in my voice I called out, "Girls...girls...let's quiet down. There's too much noise in there."

As the loud sounds tapered off Amy said, very disgustedly, "Charles, we're not girls. We're kids! Don't you know that?"

Trying to bring order out of chaos in the gym one day when it was time to line up, I said, "Come on, kids, line up now...quiet down...line up here..." (pointing to the exit door). "If you hurry and are quiet, I'll tell you a secret." (I had no idea what the secret would be, but the kids were quieting down.) So I said the first thing that came into my head, "You're a boy," pointing to a boy and repeating the comment as I went down the line, alternating with "and you're a girl," as the situation warranted. The kids seemed surprisingly impressed with this "secret," that is, most of them. When I came to Ta, the smallest child of the bunch, his response to my comment was, "I'm **not a boy...I'm a man!**" He pulled himself up on his tiptoes and looked me right in the eye. I got down on my knees, gave him a big smile and a hug. Once more on my feet, we moved out of the gym in an orderly fashion.

One of the mothers, deciding it was time her child met reality, got into this conversation with her.

Mother: "Where do you think the Easter basket came from?"

Child: "From the Easter bunny."

Mother: "Now, dear, you know what bunnies look like. How could they bring that basket?"

Child: (after a long pause and much reflection) "Well, you mean you bring it, Mommy?"

Mother: "Yes, I do."

Child: (obviously annoyed) "I'm going to forget you said that!"

It is amazing how a young child's mood will shift relatively quickly from a high, happy frame of mind, to a low, unhappy one. Judeon gave me an excellent example of this, this morning. She came in dressed in new jeans and shirt. When I commented on them favorably, she was so happy. In fact, she climbed onto my lap, hugged me and kissed me, and said, "I love you, Charles." This happened six times in ten minutes!

Then she said to me, "Charles, can I have the Play-doh?" She was so sweet and appealing.

Realizing this would entail giving the dough to several of her playmates, who would suddenly decide they needed some, also, and realizing that in ten minutes we would have to leave for our morning snack at the gym, I wasn't keen about granting her request. It just was not practical, so I said, "Well, Judeon, we don't have time now. Maybe later when we come back from the gym."

Her smile quickly changed to a scowl, and she said, with a pout, "I don't like you." Then she walked away and turned on her crying act again, very loud sounds with no tears falling.

The two of them had become so rambunctious that I just had to separate them—Dennard and Michael B. So I made Dennard sit down at one end of the table in the "all purpose room" and Michael at the other end.

Immediately Michael struggled to get up, and then he sat down again next to Dennard. Shortly thereafter the boisterous behavior of the two began again. Finally I said, "Michael, we're going to the gym in a couple of minutes. If you don't quiet down, you're going to sit and not play when we get there."

That did it. He returned to his seat scowling and saying to me, "I'll sit down, but when I get to the gym I'm going to be real nasty...watch me!" Then he sat quietly at the table and pouted.

A few minutes later we left for the gym. Once there the children exercised a lot of freedom. The noise was bearable because the room was large, but Michael kept his threat. **He was nasty! I kid you not!**

9   Charles' Hair - A Recurrent Curiosity

In order to appreciate these stories you need to know that my hair is combed over and across the top of my head from the left side. Subconsciously or otherwise, this is probably a vain attempt on my part to disguise my bald spots.

When I began working at the day care I never dreamed that my hair would become an interesting curiosity to the children. True, I was losing it, and as time wore on that became more and more apparent. Still, lots of men my age and even younger have this problem. Do they also have to contend, at times, with the feeling that somehow they are on display? Perhaps. I understand something of what they feel.

Here are a few experiences relating to my thinning locks of hair, and my associations with the children.

One day Justin was sitting on my lap, running his hand through my sparse hair. Presently, with obvious affection he said ever so sweetly, "Charles, I like your hair...'specially in the front where it uster was and s'not anymore."

At the close of another hot summer's day, Cathy, one of the teachers in the oldest group, was sitting patiently on one of the small chairs in the room. Jaime was tenderly brushing Cathy's hair. I remarked that it looked like one day maybe Cathy would be calling her hairdresser, Jaime, on a regular basis to have her hair done. Not missing a stroke with the hairbrush, Jaime smiled and said to me, "Yeah, but you won't have to worry, you're bald!"

"True," I said, with great finality.

I was on the floor playing with a group of four-year-olds. As so often happens, one of the kids couldn't resist mussing my hair and eventually commenting on the bald spots. Nicole had expressed an interest in them on more than one occasion. Today as I struggled to my feet and attempted to smooth my hair into place, Nicole said, "Charles, I know how you can make hair grow on the holes in your hair."

I thought, "Well, here goes." "How, Nicole?" I asked.

She replied in a tone of muted authority, "Just jump up and down on one foot."

After nap time one day I was on the floor helping the children with their socks and shoes. They were all milling around, trying to be "first." Michael climbed on my back and ran his hand through my hair.

Suddenly his curiosity was aroused. "Why do you cut holes in your hair?" he asked.

The attention of all the children was riveted on me as I attempted to explain. "I don't cut holes in my hair, Michael. Sometimes men lose their hair when they get older."

Michael's response was, "You lost your hair? Where did you lose it?"

Glancing around quickly, I could tell by the expressions of the boys and girls that this was a very serious question that needed to be answered very carefully. "Children," I said, "what happens is that my hair just seems to fall out."

To this reply, several asked the inevitable question, "Why?" When I said, "Oh, I don't know. It just falls out," the concerted dissatisfied looks left me in a quandary.

I silently asked myself the question, "How does one explain to three-year-olds the reasons: heredity and male hormones?" I decided to drop the subject, coward that I am, but I felt frustrated that for all my yakking, I couldn't find the right words. I silently consoled myself with the thought, "Oh well, some day they'll be old enough to understand."

Nathan is a very pleasant boy, very active, and he mingles well with the others in the class, but he doesn't have very much to say, which is why I was surprised and delighted when this happened.

The kids were rough-housing in front of the church one morning. Presently I decided I needed to sit down and rest on the steps. Several of the children came over to fool around with me while I was seated. Nathan climbed on my shoulders, hugging me all the while and obviously enjoying himself very much.

Suddenly he started mussing my hair, and then—out of the blue— he announced to me very seriously, "Boy, do you need a haircut!" As far as I can tell, that was the extent of his verbal comments to anyone the whole time I was in his presence that day.

Michael A.'s disposition for the most part was sunny, but occasionally he would feel insecure when his daddy would drop him off in the morning. At such times he would burst into tears and look anxiously around the room. One of the teachers present and in close proximity to him would then reach out to Michael and comfort him.

On one such occasion I was the one offering my arms to him. He climbed onto my lap, and I spoke soothing words to him. In a moment he was fine and smiling. He touched my head as he looked me in the eyes. and he said, "I like you, Charles. You're like my granddaddy. He doesn't have hair either."

The frequent references to my unruly hair right after a shampoo was beginning to make me self-conscious. After the fifth or sixth time of, "Charles, what happened to your hair?" and my feeble reply, "Nothing, it just looks this way whenever I wash it," I was more than touched by Ana's soft, sweet comment, "Charles, I love your hair. It's so wild."

Out of the mouths of babes!

Marita was very busy drawing a picture of a man. He appeared to have a rather large head and sparse hair. One of the teachers who had been watching Marita as she drew her picture began a conversation with her. Marita went on drawing as she responded without ever looking up from her art work. This is the conversation as I overheard it:

"Who is that a picture of, Marita?"

"My boy friend."

"Oh? What's his name?"

"Charles."

"How come he has so little hair?"

"He's bald. **He's very bald!**"

End of conversation!

10   Stuff and Nonsense

Much of each day's experiences are interwoven with moments of hilarity sparked by all sorts of things, but I guess mostly by the rich imaginations of the children. As long as we are privileged to associate with them, we can look forward to times like these.

As you read on perhaps you, too, will become happily immersed in these moments of "stuff and nonsense." Okay?

P.S. I have to confess my imagination runs in the same circle as theirs.

Pedaling her bike on the playground and stopping short, shy Ivy was overheard exclaiming, "I need some night life here!" Then she quietly moved on her way.

Alexis was commenting on her sister Amanda who had recently been ill. "Amanda had the chicken-pox, but she's back today."

"Oh," I said "I'm glad she's better, but what about you? Do you have the chicken-pox?"

"Oh no," said Alexis, "not until her spots are all gone."

"Why is that," I questioned, curious to hear what she would have to say.

Her reply was prompt and to the point. "Because that's the way it's supposed to be." I mused for a moment on the truth of this revelation.

It was "free time" again, and Sheri (just turned three) was being most demonstrative as she strutted around in her oversized high heels, long dress, and floppy hat. Then she said to an indifferent Ryan, in a manner befitting a sultry film star, "Hold me...kiss me...hug me...let's make love...let's get married." My immediate reaction, which I stifled, was, "Haven't you gotten your priorities out of order?" Is this perhaps a child's commentary on today's mores? I wonder.

Jaime, (pronounced Hymie), Ashwini (a lovely lass from India), and I were walking down the hall to the bathroom. Both children were brand new in the Child Care Center, and I felt some orientation was in order. Pointing to the appropriate room I said, "This is the girls' room, Ashwini," and then pointing to the adjoining room, I added, "And this is the boys' room, Jaime."

Jaime asked, "And where do you go to the bathroom?"

I replied, "To the boys' room. After all, I'm a man, and men go to the boys' room."

I intended to add, "you know, like all men, I'm just a grown boy," but my thoughts were tersely interrupted by Jaime, who said very seriously, "You're not a man, you're an hombre!"

Paola had the attention of a few of her fans. She was in an expansive mood and began to share some thoughts. "I saw a movie on TV where the two women were in bed kissing each other like Mommy and Daddy...a lot on the mouth," she said, her eyes rolling suggestively.

This apparently was too much for William, so he remarked with great self-assurance and a bright smile, "Oh, they were only kidding!" That stopped the conversation cold.

Recently I spontaneously invented a new game, again, a surprise as much to me as to the kids in the day care who have gotten involved with it. It started in the gym when one of the boys, Pascal, asked me again, "What's your name?"

Having told him my name the day before for at least the tenth time, I facetiously responded, "Omar Sharif."

He looked incredulously at me, not really convinced. At about that time several "rubber-necked" youngsters around us who knew my name burst into laughter. More than one of them said that my name was Charles. Then one by one they lined up, so to speak, and in turn said, "What's my name?" For replies, I resurrected the names of lots of old time movie stars and other famous persons. The list contained such gems as Pearl White, Zazu Pitts, Ramon Navarro, Peter Lorre, Helen Twelvetrees, Ben Blue, Magda Lupescu, Giovanni Martinelli, Lily Pons, Walter Damrosch, to name a few. Each name that came pouring out of my mouth was greeted with gales of laughter from a very responsive group of three-year-olds. We had a new game! We had lots of laughter! It was fun.

Each day one or more of the children would ask me, "What's my name?" And I would respond with whatever name popped into my head. Often the names are very colorful but not genuine—just figments of my imagination.

Today when I saw Alpher standing on the platform in the gym poised to jump to the mat below, I began again with, "What's your name?"

His face was bright with his beautiful smile as he responded, "ABCD. What's your name?"

I answered, "FGHI." Pausing briefly I said, "What did you say your name was?"

Immediately he said, "TKLPQ what's yours?"

Really into it now, I replied, "RSTUV" and then the inevitable, "And your name, please?"

There was a long pause, and then with a very serious look replacing his smile, there came a completely unexpected answer: "Jesus!"

Startled, I asked, "Jesus? Your name is Jesus?"

Grinning again, Alpher remarked, "Yes, you r'ember...Jesus loves me this I know."

On cue I volunteered "For the Bible tells me so." Then we began to sing the song together, his words a bit of "mish-mash" towards the end, but he was right on tune all the way. Just before we finished the last line, Alpher had jumped off the stand onto the mat, and then he ran off with great burst of energy so typical of children his age. Presently he was running happily alongside a few boys and girls in the area. It had been a joyous few moments for both of us.

Here comes Mickey on the run, all smiles. What was that she said as she rushed by? Did I hear correctly? "Your name is Roger Rabbit?"...Hm-m-m.

There is no question that Mrs. Harne, teacher for the young twos, is much loved by the children. I was reminded of this fact when I eavesdropped on the conversation of the older twos who were surrounding their flannel board. All four of the tots wanted to be the teacher at the same time-Miss Harne." It was the beginning of a battle, it seemed, as voices were rapidly rising and pushing and shoving had begun.

As I decided to break it up and moved in that direction, Danny backed off and wailed very loudly, "If I can't be Miss Harne, I don't want to play." Two others followed the lead with the same outburst and departure, leaving Tabitha by herself. Pieces of flannel were literally flying on the board as she whipped them in place and hollered instructions to the others who, no longer on the scene, were oblivious to her commands. Instead they were tumbling and wrestling on the rug in great glee.

Finally Tabitha surveyed the situation, quickly abandoned the flannel board in favor of the wrestling mat, and tumbled on top of the other three, adding to the joyful din with some outbursts of her own.

There was a traffic tie-up of blue bicycles on the blacktop of the playground. Tabitha, on the first bicycle, had this to say, "Charles, I have a bicycle at home. It has training wheels."

Pascal, second in line, with a thoughtful look on his face, immediately said, "My daddy has a new car. It has training wheels." Then Tabitha pulled away followed by Pascal and then Raphael, on the third bike. I was left sitting on the truck tire and wondering if this conversation really took place.

Raphael was up and down from a chair, and he paced back and forth in the room, occasionally hiccupping. When he noticed that several of us were watching, he stopped, smiled mischievously, and then said, "There's a monster inside me." He hiccupped. "See...there he goes again." And he took off, all smiles.

In the gym Dennard came up to me and obviously wanted some TLC. In fact, he asked to sit on my lap, which I encouraged. He began sucking his finger. Then with a bright smile and a sweeping gesture, he started rubbing my face with his wet finger.

"Oh, Dennard," I said, "don't do that. That's not nice. It's like putting spit on my face."

With that he began to massage his face with the same finger, saying ever so sweetly, "That's not spit, that's lotion."

Where, oh where does he get those ideas?

I guess it was inevitable. I was horsing around with the two and three-year olds in the gym, and we were close to one of the mats. Suddenly a group of nine, five boys and four girls—succeeded in getting me down on the mat after tugging at my legs. Once I was on the mat, they were rolling all over me.

In all this confusion, Shena, an observer of the situation, came up to me and said very casually, "Charles, when you have a minute, will you help me find a ball I can play with?"

Still struggling to get out from under, and obviously losing ground, I said desperately, "How about tomorrow? Maybe I'll be free then!"

Shena's quick response was, "Okay." Then she jumped into the fray.

I thought, "Maybe the fire alarm will go off, or Amy will come back from the bathroom." "Amy," I called...then louder, "Amy...Amy, I need you!"

Dennard has a very bad habit of ignoring his nose when it needs blowing. We can't always tell that he has such a need. Instead, the need becomes evident when, after a loud sneeze, we hear strange sounds coming from him. Inevitably we'll see him standing in a panic, with his nose erupting like a volcano. Then we rush to him with a Kleenex box in hand.

When his nose gave evidence of this kind of trouble after a big sneeze today, I said in an exasperated voice, "Why don't you blow your nose when it needs to be blown instead of waiting until you have a big sneeze?"

As I began ministering to this need with Kleenex after Kleenex, he rolled those big expressive eyes at me and said, "Okay, Mama."

Terrell, one of the boys in the four/five-year-old class, is not one of our best sleepers at naptime. In fact, he rarely sleeps. Instead his mind seems to be going all the time. Being a "mass observer" he never misses anything that is going on.

One day I was in the room when the kids were bedded down, and an hour had passed. Terrell was tossing and turning, asking questions, calling for Kleenex—his usual pattern of behavior at naptime. I was reading a book. Presently Terrell began this routine:

"Charles, Charles."

My prompt response was "Sh...sh! Sh...sh!"

But Terrell continued.

"Charles, Charles."

And I responded each time a little more loudly. Finally in desperation I said (not softly, I'm afraid) "What is it, Terrell?"

His response was, "Why are you wearing ladies' stockings, Charles?"

I looked down at my dull, drab, tan nylon socks and said, "These are not ladies' stockings. They are men's nylon socks."

"They look like ladies' stockings to me," he replied.

I walked briskly over to the side of his cot, raised my pants legs, and showed him my socks. "They're ladies' stockings," he said, "I know. My mother sometimes wears them short like that."

I sighed deeply, and almost in disgust I said, "Go to sleep, Terrell."

Returning to my chair I glanced quickly in his direction. From the look on his face it was very obvious he was convinced he was right, and I was weird in my choice of socks...or should I say "stockings?"

Jennifer had been naughty and was sitting on the floor sulking. She seemed so blue that I thought I needed to encourage her. I went over to her, knelt down, put my arm around her, and began to speak soft words of encouragement to her. She pouted even more and then suddenly blurted out, "Don't touch my body!" Abashed, I instinctively backed off. And then as though she felt she might have gone too far, she added almost sweetly, "Just touch my legs." I stifled the urge to grin and instead murmured something innocuous to dispel my embarrassment.

I was having another fun time with the two/three-year-old children in the gym on an afternoon when the inclement weather precluded our going out. I decided to try my "whispering nonsense comments into the ears of the children." The object, of course, was twofold: (1) to get their reactions and (2) to see if they could follow instructions. I explained that whatever I whispered, they were to whisper to the child next to them. (We were seated on the platform of the slide.) So I began as follows:

Charles (to Marcus), "Butchie was eating Play-doh."

Marcus (smiling): "He was?"

We had a problem, but I almost expected we would. When I tried other comments to other children—like Andrew who was to relay the message to Jennifer, or Butchie who was to repeat to Marcus—I got either dead silence or a verbal response. It was obvious the repetition concept was too difficult for them. When I finally suggested we try another game, I was bombarded with the usual outbursts, "No, no. My turn, my turn."

So we compromised, as I said simply "Okay I'll whisper in your ears something about one of the children." There was immediate agreement. We began again:

Charles to Sean: "Amanda is a mess."

Sean: (grinning) "I know...I know."

There were later responses to my other nonsense remarks, but this one stayed with me somehow.

Jason, one of the more "active" boys and also one of the more adventuresome, seemed to be playing rather quietly—most unusual for him. He was riding a bike in the gym very carefully and seriously. Out of curiosity and perhaps with a touch of facetiousness, I said, "Jason, are you okay? You're awfully quiet today."

His immediate response was, "No, I don't feel well. Can't you tell? I'm not getting into trouble." Then he pedaled away.

11 Miscellaneous - Philosophical and Otherwise

The use of the word "otherwise" in the title of this chapter may sound like a "cop-out" to you. But don't forget, this is the last chapter, and I'm trying to fit in my stories that didn't seem to belong elsewhere. Furthermore, I already used the word "miscellaneous" in my title, and I don't want to be called redundant. Heaven forbid! So-o-o let us begin!

Reflections

July 1, 1988 - I'm dating this comment because something happened today in the day care that really made me "situp and take notice," as the saying goes. We had a visitor who I recognized immediately...Paola! She is nine-years-old now, quite "grown up," and even more interesting than when she was a part of our school. And she's going into the fourth grade! It seems like just yesterday that she graduated from the Day Care, aged five! She, along with others in her group and some earlier, are mentioned in this book. That means the book has been in the process of conception for more than six years! And I still have not finished compiling, editing, typing, etc.

Most of the time after a sharp verbal exchange with a child you can renew your relationship with him or her. This could be the same day or the next, kind of like wiping the slate clean. As Christians we are taught that this is how God deals with us when we are penitent of our sins, and He forgives us. He not only forgives, he forgets! That's the way little children are. Surely we can be no less.

Spontaneous stories told to children can sometimes boomerang. For example, I often make up stories that may be a bit wild, if not weird, in their details. In the next day or two after such a story, one or more children will ask me to repeat the story. They are frustrated when I can't recall all the details which, for some reason unknown to me, they can recall. Sometimes then the stories end up being told by the children to me, and often I don't recognize them. At the very least they and I feel frustrated at this point.

Maxine, our day care director at one time, was telling the children a Bible story without any written notes and only a colorful illustrative picture for a prop. The group was very interested and impressed. Terrell was especially smitten with the story. When it was over he asked, "How did you do that?"

Maxine's response was, "I did it with my mind."

Terrell was still confused, and he asked again, "But how did you do it? Where's your book?"

Maxine's remark, "In my head," really didn't seem to clear up the matter for Terrell.

So he said, "Yes...but..." Maxine explained that she had read the story many times, so she remembered it. His continued, amazed look indicated he thought she was very remarkable.

Maxine, after a session of trying firmly but in love to quiet the children, wanting to have their attention, finally said, "You know, there have to be rules and regulations in this world. Parents and teachers don't always like to fuss at their children. Your daddies sometimes have to shake you or spank you when you keep on being naughty and don't obey the rules."

Kimberly sighed and said, "I know what you mean. A man has to do what he has to do!" The group of children nodded and murmured their approval of her comment. And the nice thing about it was that it became quiet again.

Tabitha made it quite clear that she didn't particularly like Ashley...not in so many words but in her overall attitude toward him. She avoided him and moved away from him whenever he got too close to her. And the succession of glares she bestowed on him were really pretty bad.

For some reason Ashley was tantalized by her rebuffs. He tried in many ways to please her. For instance, when they were at the same work table he shared his crayons with her. At lunch time when passing out the napkins he always gave her the first one. Once outside on the playground I saw him get off his bike when she passed close to him, and he offered it to her. She grabbed it roughly and rode off without so much as a word...even when I called to her, "What do you say, Tabitha?"

But Ashley persisted in his positive overtures. He seemed determined to get in her good graces. I admired his resoluteness. Today I watched as Ashley walked up to Tabitha. You could almost feel her bristling when she realized he was near her. If he noticed her negativeness, he never let on. Instead in the sweetest of voices he said, "I love you, Tabitha."

Her voice was gruff as she hurled her reply, "Oh, gross!" Then she walked guickly away. Ashley was crushed. He turned and looked so sadly in her direction. I thought about speaking to him and to Tabitha, but you know, I really didn't know what to say.

After naptime one day as I was stacking the cots and ushering the kids to and from the bathrooms, I proceeded to nudge Nelia who was still snoozing. Sleepily, she finally dragged herself out of her cot. She had tossed and turned and moved her blanket from one side to another and was the last to fall asleep. It had been quite a workout for her before she drifted off to sleep.

I always try to make a comment for each child, conscious that they are all listening to hear what will be said. I was running out of ideas, but I couldn't help but notice how disheveled Nelia's sheet was. Before I knew it, I blurted out, "Nelia, your bed is a mess. It looks like you've been sleeping in it." The room exploded with laughter. As corny as my remark was to me, the kids seemed to love it...even Nelia!

I had to come to the Center that morning about 8:15. You see, I had agreed to be the cook for that day, and I needed plenty of time to get the morning snacks ready, not to mention the lunch.

Mid-morning the two-year-olds were playing in the gym right outside the kitchen. Marco spied me with my apron on, very engrossed in my work. Finally he entered the kitchen and approached me timidly. I looked up, gave him a big smile, and said, "Can I help you, Marco?"

There was a studied silence before he asked, "Charles, are you a girl?"

I laughed and said, "No, of course not."

Still puzzled he asked, "Then how come you cook?" I mentioned something to the effect that men are able to cook, too. I could tell by the way he looked at me that he didn't buy that!

Sometimes adults supply an amusing anecdote, as witness this one. Joey had been almost the ideal child for a day care. He was quiet, reserved, good-looking, cooperative, obedient, dependable, and very interesting. On the other hand, his younger brother Timmy was always a challenge. He was noisy, unreserved, good-looking, inclined to be uncooperative, often disobedient, dependable—in the sense you knew he'd come through with a mischievous deed—and also very interesting. Joey had moved on to grade school.

One day Timmy's dad brought Tim to the Center. Spontaneously I greeted him, "Hi, Joey! How are you?" His dad smiled and said, "That's Timmy."

"Oh yes," was my reply, calling down the hall to the gentleman as he went in to the adjoining room, "I guess you'd call that a Freudian slip."

A moment later Timmy's dad came in to give Timmy a last bear hug before he left for work. "Goodbye, Joey, be a good boy. See you later." I had picked up on that right away, and then Timmy's dad realized what he had said. Smiling broadly, he remarked, "Another Freudian slip!" We laughed. He turned and left, and I ushered Timmy in the direction of his already noisy friends, busy at play.

Out of a clear blue sky Percy said to me, "I saw a man kiss a girl on TV."

Percy seemed anxious about this, so I asked, "Well, did that make you nervous?"

With a sheepish look on his face, he said, "No, it really didn't make me nervous. I thought it was funny."

A group of children were responding to my remark, "Mirror, mirror on the wall, who is the fairest of them all?" All the girls in the group shouted, "Me!" By contrast, none of the boys said anything, but it was obvious they approved of the girls' responses. Can it be that they understand, already, that in our culture only girls are "fair?" I couldn't help wondering, "How do they refer to themselves?"

Amanda had left our day care center upon her graduation and had enrolled at another center. Sometime later, one of our staff ran into Amanda's mother. They exchanged remarks and updated one another. Then Amanda's mother shared a delightful story about Amanda at her new center.

Shortly after she was introduced to an aide, the teacher doing the introducing explained how helpful the aide was. This was a puzzle to Amanda. That evening she said to her mother, "We have an aide in our room, and I'm scared of her."

"Why, Amanda?" asked her curious mother. Her response was, "Well, didn't you say that Aids can kill people?"

Emily was sitting next to me at lunch time on a particularly difficult Monday. It seems the children are often the wildest and most unmanageable on Mondays. Today it had been hard to get them quiet even for the blessing before the meal began. Suddenly Emily looked up to me and with that peculiar voice of hers, reminiscent of Fanny Brice as Baby Snooks, she said, "I don't know if I'm going to be able to get through this day!" She looked so woe-be-gone. Somehow I managed to keep it to myself, but all I could think of was, "If you think you're having a bad day, wait until you get to be my age, and a day like today comes your way!"

Recently Tyria, very perturbed, came running up to me in the gym. "Carlos spit at me," she whined.

"And what did you do to make him spit at you?" I asked. "You must have done something." Tyria remained silent. "What did you do first, Tyria?" I asked somewhat insistent.

After a long pause and apparently some reflection on her part, she responded sheepishly, "I spit at him." She walked away, obviously chagrined. I felt encouraged.

One afternoon when I arrived at the day care, it was obvious to me from the way Erica greeted me, that her experience of having been bitten by one of the boys made quite an indelible impression on her mind. Apparently the incident proved to be not only painful but a bit mystifying as well. Oh, she didn't use those words, of course, but what she did say and how she said it conveyed those thoughts to me.

"Michael bit me," she exclaimed as she ran toward me. There was pain in her expression, and she started crying.

Instinctively I knelt down to comfort her.

"I'm sorry," I said. "Why did he do that?"

With an incredulous look on her face she responded, "I don't know...and it hurt." She rubbed the spot on her chest.

And so the story went with each "new" person who arrived on the scene. And always there was the mystery of it all when she was questioned, "Why?" But the moment of truth finally came when Erica's mother showed up at the gym to pick her up. Erica ran, crying that Michael had bitten her. While her mother hugged her and examined the wound, it was as though Erica was waiting for the inevitable question. It finally came. "Why did Michael bite you, Erica?" asked her mother.

Instantly came the response, "Because he's an old grouch." And the tears flowed once more.

One morning at the day care, a four-year-old child was talking about her exciting weekend, sharing the details with an interested few of her companions. Wishing to reflect my interest, also, I asked her, "Did you enjoy being a flower girl?" "Oh yes," she answered, "I got to wear a pretty pink dress, but my aunt who was getting married...her dress was only white."

Amy and I were trying to get the kids ready to go outside. Devin was uncooperative, however. He was engaged in what to me seemed like a game, bouncing up and down and "bopping" first this child then that one.

After several attempts to keep him seated with the other children, who would occasionally imitate his actions, in exasperation I said, "Devin, I told you four times to stay seated, and you're still jumping up. If I speak to you again, you'll have to sit when we go out instead of playing."

Then I sat him down again as he was saying, "I'll be good. I'll be good."

A moment later he was on his feet. "Devin!" I yelled.

He quickly sat down. Meekly he said to me, "I guess I better pray about this."

"You better," I snapped. He closed his eyes, folded his hands and bowed his head. From where I was sitting his lips seemed to be moving, but if he was praying, I couldn't say. Only God knows.

Martine, an older three-year-old, and I were involved in a "serious" discussion in the gym. It started out with comments about the wagon, the popular toy at the time. At one point, I said, "Oh yes, when I was a child I used to like to play with a wagon, too."

There was a brief pause, but then Martine asked me, "Were you a boy or a girl?"

Startled, I replied briskly, "I was a boy, of course."

She looked amazed and said, "Why?"

Sucking in my breath I exclaimed, "When a boy grows up he becomes a man. When a girl grows up she becomes a woman."

Looking at me as if I had said something earthshaking she asked, "But, why?"

"Because that is how God made us."

I joined in her reply, "Why?"

I had run out of explanations. I felt myself growing impatient also. So I picked up a large, red rubber ball and dribbled it a few feet, turned, and tossed it to Martine. When she responded in kind I hummed to myself, "And the Band Played On."

Sometimes a tired teacher who is running out of patience contributes a quotable comment. Here's one. Carson was poking around and taking her time in the bathroom. Her teacher, Iris, was fidgeting and anxious to get Carson back to the room. Suddenly Iris raised her voice in exasperation, "Hurry up, Carson. You're not washing away your sins. You're just washing your hands!" I got a real chuckle out of that one.

I was present when the oldest class was together for a time of sharing and activity. One of the girls said very proudly, "I'm four years old." Immediately another said, "I'm five." Soon it seemed each child was spouting his or her age. During a lull I asked, tongue in cheek, "How old do you think I am?"

The room quieted down more so, and a boy said, "Are you six?" There were a few giggles, and one girl said, "Of course not. Charles is older than that."

"Well," I smiled encouragingly, "How old am I then?"

She hemmed and hawed and said hesitatingly, "Eight?" My response was in the negative. Then after some deep thought she said, "I know. You're twelve!"

Everyone seemed to be impressed, and not wishing to cut her down again, I said, "Well, not exactly, but you're getting there." She smiled and the subject seemed to be ended.

Have you ever noticed when a child has something he or she is enjoying, frequently another child just has to have that object? Often you are called on to help out. For instance, check on this dialogue. Doesn't it sound familiar?

Shari: (to Charles), "I want to hold Heather's pumpkin book."

Charles: "Why don't you say to Heather, 'May I hold your pumpkin book, please?'"

Shari: "May I hold your pumpkin book, please?"

Heather: (nastily) "No!"

Shari grabbed the book out of Heather's hands and hurried off to enjoy it. Heather seemed quite startled...yes, even speechless.

Near the close of a difficult day, it suddenly occurred to me that Daniel's dad had been watching me trying to referee several clashes between different children in the large room. I turned around at one point and noticed him staring at us all in a bewildered manner.

As Daniel rushed over to his dad, who had come to pick him up, with a sigh and a smile I said to his father, "It's been a long day."

His response was, "Charles, why would you volunteer for this job?" I shrugged my shoulders and smiled again, saying, "I guess it's because I love these kids."

As he and Daniel left he shook his head and said, "You're really something!" On that particularly rough day I needed and appreciated that affirmation, believe me.

Epilogue

In this book I have tried to share the happy, exuberant, thoughtful conduct of children and for the most part, not report on their unhappy, difficult experiences. I hope I have not conveyed the impression that being a day care teacher is a bed of roses, for we teachers, as well as the children, have our bad days. How we cope with the "difficult" days is a reflection on our training, experience, and patience and as such is not the subject of this book.

Youngsters tend to reflect the influences of their environment in their behavior. Educators will tell you that children may imitate their elders in their play. In addition to happy experiences in their home spilling over into their conduct at the day care, their frustrations and hurts sometimes explode at the center. These are often unexpected by the classmates or teachers.

Many of our children come from broken homes or single parent homes where, to say the least, they may experience various kinds of pain, frustrations, and sadness. Likewise, it is obvious to us that often a parent experiences guilt about the necessity of placing his or her child in a day care. Sometimes this leads to a child being showered with expensive presents or lavished with other kinds of attention that might be considered excessive for the child—perhaps evidence of spoiling the child. Hence, additional frustrating pressures are building up for the parent, not to mention the child's growing expectations of receiving more and more of such attention. It is inevitable that all these pressures are bound to effect the child.

On any given day then, some of our day care teachers have to deal with revelations of anger, hurt, and rebellion of the children, sometimes shown in their violent resistance to rules and regulations. How do you tell a child, for instance, when he is in rebellion that the rules of the day care are enforced for the overall benefit of the center? Obviously, he neither understands or cares, he's just hurting.

At such times the teachers are called upon to handle the disturbing experiences in an authoritative, but hopefully loving manner. But like children who are imperfect, we, too, show our imperfections. It would be naive on our part to ignore that education takes place even when the immature child seeks, in his or her own way, to cope with all the pressures at home and at the school. We are constantly challenged to remember all these things and to reflect on the individual child and his or her problems.

With these brief, perhaps incomplete and inadequate comments, suffice it to say each day is begun with the teachers' determination to handle all situations well. And we try...we really do, but in retrospect, too often we are reminded or remind ourselves that we might have done better. In the future, with God's help, we may.